Ancient Egypt

Discovering its Splendors

Ancient Egypt
Discovering its Splendors

NATIONAL
GEOGRAPHIC
SOCIETY

Ancient Egypt

Discovering its Splendors

Published by
The National Geographic Society

Melvin M. Payne
Chairman of the Board

Robert E. Doyle
President

Owen R. Anderson
Secretary

Melville Bell Grosvenor
Editor Emeritus

Gilbert M. Grosvenor
Editor

A volume in the
Story of Man Library
Prepared by
National Geographic
Book Service
Jules B. Billard, *Director*

Chapters by

Karl W. Butzer
Virginia Lee Davis
I. E. S. Edwards
Barbara Mertz
William H. Peck
Edna R. Russmann
William Kelly Simpson
Anthony J. Spalinger

Staff for this Book

Jules B. Billard
Editor

Charles O. Hyman
Art Director

Anne Dirkes Kobor
Illustrations Editor

Mary H. Dickinson
Chief Researcher

Thomas B. Allen
Ross S. Bennett
Seymour L. Fishbein
Mary Swain Hoover
Edward Lanouette
David F. Robinson
Verla Lee Smith
Editor-Writers

Carol Bittig Lutyk
Shirley L. Scott
Elizabeth C. Wagner
Editorial Research

Robert C. Firestone
Production Manager

Karen F. Edwards
Assistant Production Manager

Molly Kohler
Illustrations Research

Victor R. Boswell, Jr.,
and Farrell Grehan
Photography

John T. Dunn
William W. Smith
Engraving and Printing

Suzanne P. Kane
Lise Swinson
Assistants

George I. Burneston, III
Index

Contributions by
Thomas J. Abercrombie
Constance Brown Boltz
Effie M. Cottman
Margaret Deane Gray
John D. Garst, Jr.
Michael A. Hampshire
David M. Seager
George E. Stuart
Lloyd K. Townsend, Jr.
Anne E. Withers

326 illustrations,
306 in full color

First edition 425,000 copies
Library of Congress CIP Data Page 256

Pages 2-3: Shadowed by a winter
sunset, the pyramids of Chephren
(right) and Mycerinus at Giza
evoke the enduring fascination
of ancient Egypt—land of sun
and sky and mighty splendor.
Page 7: Desert hills edge the west
bank of the Nile near Aswan, where
the river's First Cataract marked
ancient Egypt's southern frontier.

Contents

Foreword

Day after day through chill winter months the line of people snaked around the block from the building's entrance. For four, six, and as much as ten hours, men, women, and children waited as the queue inched into the National Gallery of Art in Washington, D. C. Enterprising sidewalk vendors did land-office businesses selling coffee, hot chocolate, and sandwiches—even knitted wool caps—to the patient throngs. What was the attraction that drew so many? The treasures of Tutankhamun, from the Egyptian Museum in Cairo, which we at the National Gallery had the privilege of starting on a seven-city tour of the United States.

From November to March nearly 7,000 persons a day wound into the rooms where 55 priceless pieces from the boy-king's tomb were shown. Visitors were drawn from miles away—altogether a number larger than the entire population of the District of Columbia. The crowds taxed the National Gallery's facilities in surprising ways—for example, we had to put a man to work cleaning air filters full time just to keep up with the dust that came in with the people.

The same enthusiastic acceptance greeted the Tutankhamun exhibit in the other cities where it was shown. The public's response became a powerful tribute to the sheer visual quality of the pieces, and to the fascination of their breathtaking age, the drama of their discovery, and the ancient Egyptian's obsession with life's ability to transcend death.

These thoughts and scenes came back as I leafed through page proofs of this book. And I was carried back to the sun-drenched days of my own first trip to Egypt, taken when I was a student at the Louvre in Paris and studying with the great Egyptologist Christiane Desroches-Noblecourt. The impact of the monuments in their settings was as great as any artistic experience I have ever had: the forms straining toward the sun, as pyramids or obelisks; or flattened lizard-like against the stone in relief; and in Cairo's Egyptian Museum, the taut elegance, purity, and restraint of objects made a thousand years before Tutankhamun.

Egypt has offered our civilization so much more than the treasures of Tutankhamun, dazzling as they are. The book for which I write these words makes that point in an eloquent way. Created under the guiding hand of a friend of many years, William Kelly Simpson, the eminent Yale Egyptologist and curator of Egyptian art at the Boston Museum of Fine Arts, it tells the story of a great civilization in very human terms.

Outstanding scholars have contributed the text to the volume. They trace the origins of the people who launched a nation at a time when the rest of the world was hardly more than a collection of city-states. They tell how those enduring wonders of time, the pyramids, may have been built—and why. They recount how religion interwove itself in the daily activities of pharaoh and noble and peasant, shaping their expectations in the life they lived and the afterworld to come. They unfold the painstaking drudgery—and the rewards—of archeological finds, the detective work of deciphering the hieroglyphs that have helped reveal more about ancient Egypt than we know about any other civilization of that long-ago time.

The quality of the color photography is the envy of all of us who have ever held a camera. The ancient Egyptians were intensely visual; even their writing was visually based, and the imagery of their poetry bears this out. I believe they would have loved this book. I know of no other book on the Egypt of the pharaohs that presents its treasures and its grandeur with this visual quality, and with such impressive scale.

To the fortunate reader I can only wish the injunction carved on the white lotus goblet in the Tutankhamun exhibition: "May your *ka* [spirit] live and may you spend millions of years, you who love Thebes, sitting with your face to the north wind, your two eyes beholding happiness."

The Constant Lure

William H. Peck

*Concerning Egypt itself I shall
extend my remarks to a great length,
because there is no country that
possesses so many wonders.*
                    Herodotus

*I had seen a hundred things, while a
thousand others had escaped me; and
had, for the first time, found access
to the archives of the arts and sciences.*
                    Vivant Denon

Two travelers separated in time by 2,250 years—one from the fifth century B.C., the other from the 19th century A.D.—sound a common chord. Egypt is a land of so many wonderful things the mind can hardly encompass them. The sheer quantity of remains from the past exists because the country's dry climate preserves. Man has been the worst destroyer.

What has made Egypt, its culture, and its monuments a source of fascination throughout the ages? The country resembles no other in the world. The physical situation of the land—cut off, protected, and isolated from its neighbors by mountains, desert, and sea—made it an ideal nurturing place for a unique civilization. The regularity of the Nile River floods provided a way of life that seems to have been almost changeless. Egypt has always been a land of mystery to the non-Egyptian, its monuments a source of more inspired fantasy than those of any other country. Nowhere else is there such a long, continuous tradition revealed by preserved structures, which, by their nature, seem somehow on a more than human scale.

"Egyptian king . . . receive my salutation"

Facing the life-giving Nile, a massive statue of Amunhotep III embodies the majesty of Egypt's pharaohs. Standing in western Thebes, it is one of a pair that guarded the king's mortuary temple, destroyed ages ago. Greek travelers named the northern colossus Memnon in honor of a Trojan war hero; generations of tourists engraved it with greetings and commemorative verses.

The systematic study of Egypt's past had to wait until the late 18th century when foreign scientists began to arrive. But travelers in every age tried to make sense of the mysterious country. The first students of Egypt were the Egyptians themselves. We know this because we can still read a number of graffiti scratched on monuments in pharaonic times. A tourist who visited Djoser's Step Pyramid at Saqqara a thousand years after the pharaoh's reign wrote: "The scribe, Ahmose, son of Iptah, came to see the temple of Djoser. He found it as though heaven were within it, Re rising in it." Another visitor recorded that he was on a holiday in Memphis and wanted to amuse himself. Then he added a pious prayer, which he hoped would benefit him in the afterlife.

The Egyptians knew their country to be one of great antiquity. They pondered a tradition that stretched back thousands of years. In the Song of the Harper, carved on a tomb wall, the ancient author wonders about the disappearance of the tombs of famous men:

*Their walls are dismantled,
And their cult places exist no more,
As if they had never been.*

In the seventh century B.C. the Greeks had established regular contact with Egypt. They became fascinated with the temples and tombs that still remained along the banks of the Nile. By the sixth century Greek mercenaries serving under Pharaoh Psamtik II had left graffiti at Abu Simbel, more than 600 miles from the sea. In the western Delta, the town of Naucratis was founded as a Greek trading enclave on Egyptian soil.

Persia ruled Egypt in the fifth century B.C., when the Greek historian Herodotus visited the Nile Valley. His delightful account of the trip combines hearsay, myth, and personal observation. Describing Egyptian customs, he tells us they were opposite to those practiced by the rest of the known world: "The women attend the markets and trade, while the men sit at home at the loom. . . . In other countries the priests have long hair,

9

"Soldiers, forty centuries look down upon you"

Napoleon, one of countless invaders of Egypt, pointed to the Giza pyramids as he uttered these words. Although his soldiers would know defeat, success crowned the efforts of scholars who joined the expedition. Here they measure the Sphinx, a human-headed lion that served as a guardian spirit. Medieval Moslems chiseled away the statue's nose. The French were eager sightseers—even Napoleon's aging officers, egged on by the young general's taunts, scaled the Great Pyramid and shared a little brandy at the summit.

in Egypt their heads are shaven. . . . other men pass their lives separate from animals, the Egyptians have animals always living with them. . . . When they write or calculate, instead of going, like the Greeks, from left to right, they move their hand from right to left."

Herodotus visited the pyramids and apparently became the gullible victim of a tour guide. He tells us with confidence that an inscription on the Great Pyramid, read to him by an interpreter, reveals the amount of onions and garlic consumed by the workmen who built it. And he repeats an old story—that when the pharaoh needed money to continue building, he put his daughter to work as a prostitute. The pyramid's casing stones, carried off long ago by the Arabs, probably never bore any inscriptions except graffiti.

Manetho, a high priest in the temple at Heliopolis in the third century B.C., prepared a history of Egypt that still influences historians. The document no longer exists intact, but pieces of it have been assembled from extracts found in other ancient writings. Manetho divided Egyptian history into 30 dynasties—groups of hereditary rulers—a scheme we still use, though details are missing. We wonder, for example, why one dynasty replaced another. When the French scholar Champollion deciphered the Egyptian language in the early 19th century, Manetho's lists could be compared to inscriptions on monuments, and his history turned out to be far more reliable than anyone had supposed.

To bring order to 3,000 years of history, Egyptologists divide Manetho's numbered dynasties into several phases. They designate the three great periods of Egyptian history the Old Kingdom, the Middle Kingdom, and the New Kingdom, with each followed by an Intermediate Period of political unrest. They also modified Manetho's list by adding a 31st dynasty.

Each of the three kingdoms can be characterized by certain accomplishments. Old Kingdom pharaohs raised the pyramids at the edge of the western desert. Middle Kingdom pharaohs consolidated power by controlling the nobles. The New Kingdom ushered in

"A fit prison-house for fallen angels"

Napoleon's savants explore by torchlight the cavernous Grand Gallery deep in the heart of the Great Pyramid. The sloping aisle, walled in polished limestone, stretches 153 feet and rises 28 feet to a stepped roof. The Frenchman on the ladder (opposite) disappears into a hole that leads to a compartment directly above the burial chamber—where Cheops's sarcophagus stands empty. The first visitors—robbers—came in pharaonic times; the curious have been drawn to the monument's eerie interior for centuries. Huge bats and a terrible stench greeted medieval visitors—an Arab doctor fainted from fright in a dark passage. To Victorian novelist Harriet Martineau the pyramid was a gloomy prison, but she hitched up her long skirts and climbed to the King's Chamber.

the nation's zenith as a military power. Culture and the arts flourished. At the end of the New Kingdom, about 1100 B.C., Egypt began to decline. It saw a brief renaissance with the Saite Dynasty, but felt the battering of wave after wave of invaders—culminating in the conquest by Alexander the Great in 332 B.C. Three centuries of domination by Macedonian and Ptolemaic kings ended with the country's fall to Rome in 30 B.C.

With the Roman occupation, Egypt became a thoroughly administered Roman province. Travelers could come and go in safety, using the excellent post roads maintained for the imperial mail service. Emperors and senators arrived to inspect the principal tourist attractions and to study the quaint customs of the Egyptians, who continued to live, work, and worship in the age-old way. The emperor Hadrian not only traveled in Egypt but also founded a city on the Nile. When he returned home, he ordered part of his villa at Tivoli designed Egyptian-style.

In Roman times, travelers stopped at the Giza pyramids and the Sphinx, then traveled upriver to Memphis to see the sacred bull at the Apis sanctuary. The Faiyum oasis had more attractions—the Labyrinth, a maze-like temple complex named by the Greeks for the legendary structure in Crete, and nearby, the pool of the sacred crocodile.

Thebes, capital of Egypt at the height of its power, was a ruined city even in those days, but the tourists admired the damaged temples and hiked the rocky trail to the Valley of the Kings, burial place of New Kingdom pharaohs. Most tombs had already been plundered when the Romans crawled inside and scratched their names on the walls by torchlight.

Roman emperors, who considered Egypt their personal preserve, collected antiquities on a grand scale. They carted off hundreds of statues and other objects to decorate their capital. But it was the tall obelisk, topped by a small pyramid and chiseled with mysterious hieroglyphs, that the Romans most fancied. Obelisks were dedicated to the sun god and inscribed

with names of pharaohs; the foreigners, however,
knew nothing of this. Pliny the Elder believed the inscriptions interpreted "the operations of Nature according to the philosophy of the Egyptians." Today
more obelisks stand in Rome than in Egypt. Others are
scattered about the world from New York to Istanbul.

During the Middle Ages, the association of Jewish
and Christian history with Egypt gave Europeans a
new motive for visiting. They made the journey not as
traders or tourists, but as pious pilgrims. Old Testament stories about Joseph in Egypt, the bondage of the
Israelites, the Exodus, and the New Testament account
of the Holy Family's flight from Herod made Egypt a
place of consuming interest.

Travel grew difficult and dangerous after the Arab
conquest about A.D. 640, when Egypt became part of
the Moslem world. A long silence settled over the
country during this period. The Arabs, who felt dis-
dain for a culture so alien to their own, searched the
temples and pyramids for treasure and used them as
quarries for building stone. Not until a thousand years
after the last hieroglyphs were written could Europeans travel in safety again. By that time no one understood the ancient writings. Scholars had not forgotten
the Nile Valley—the works of ancient authors were still
available. But they could shed no light on current conditions, and the country remained terra incognita.

Most of the adventurers who braved the sea voyage
or the overland route along the eastern Mediterranean
were German, French, and English. Some wrote accounts of their travels. In 1547 Pierre Belon entered the
Great Pyramid at Giza and saw the royal sarcophagus.
So did André Thevet, chaplain to Catherine de Medici,
in 1549. Thevet entered the so-called "mummy pits" at
Saqqara, looking for the bodies of dead Egyptians. The
shriveled corpses excited a great deal of interest, for by
the 16th century, "mummy" had become a popular
drug found in apothecary shops all over Europe.
Tombs were ransacked to supply the constant demand
for mummies. The Egyptians themselves broke up

Assault on Egypt's past

A steady stream of antiquities left Egypt in the 19th century, many hauled off by the great plunderer, Giovanni Belzoni. This titan of Herculean strength loaded the seven-ton head of Ramses II (right) on rollers and had it dragged nearly three miles to the Nile. From there it was shipped to the British Museum. Belzoni's Egyptian helpers accused him of using magic spells to accomplish the impossible. As the Egyptians took control of their treasures, the pillage tapered off.
The United States acquired an obelisk in 1881, when "Cleopatra's Needle," a gift of the khedive, was erected in New York's Central Park. Once it stood before the Temple of the Sun at Heliopolis.

mummy cases for firewood and sold the powdered bodies of their ancestors as medicine. "Mummy is become merchandise," wrote physician-author Sir Thomas Browne in 1658, ". . . and Pharaoh is sold for balsams." At a time when the going price in Scotland was eight shillings a pound, one canny trader exported 600 pounds in one shipment—and made a killing.

The word mummy comes from the Arabic *mumiyah*, meaning bitumen. Early Near Eastern peoples used bitumen to heal wounds. Sometimes the shiny black resins found in embalmed bodies, and even the mummy itself, were used as substitutes. If the real thing were unobtainable, the cadavers of slaves or prisoners were treated with bitumen and sold instead.

In the 11th century, the Persian physician Avicenna prescribed mummy for almost every ill—paralysis, epilepsy, nausea, ulcers, concussions, and palpitations of the heart. As late as the 1800's Arabs were still mixing mummy powder with butter as a remedy for bruises. Even today, genuine Egyptian mummy, it is rumored, can be purchased in certain New York drugstores—for forty dollars an ounce.

The curio dealers of Cairo could supply the 17th-century visitor with a complete mummy or a variety of other objects, such as amulets, scarabs, and papyri. What the Egyptians couldn't find in the desert sands they made themselves. In 1635 Archbishop Laud presented to the Bodleian Library at Oxford University one of the oldest known Egyptian fakes—a small mummiform statue, not in the least ancient. The art of faking, it seems, is as old as the tourist industry that creates a market for copies.

By the 18th century, the trickle of visitors threatened to become a torrent. Some travelers searched for antiquities to take back to collectors or museums, others were curious antiquarians who wandered from temple to temple, copying inscriptions, admiring reliefs.

If we could transport ourselves back to the Egypt of

1737, we would see a *dahabeah*—a lateen-rigged sailing vessel—moving slowly up the Nile. Aboard would be an Anglican clergyman, Richard Pococke. He had already visited Lower (northern) Egypt and was on his way to Aswan in Upper (southern) Egypt. Pococke adopted the name Yusef, let his beard grow, and wore native costume—all prudent precautions for a foreigner on the Nile. "I provided everything as for a long voyage," he wrote, "coffee, rice, tobacco, soap, red shoes of the Arabs, and several other things for presents, and took care to have sufficient arms for our defence."

At Saqqara, he had stayed in the house of a local sheikh. The Arab villagers were suspicious of foreigners and considered them fair game. Returning unexpectedly from the tombs one day, Pococke was surprised by an eight-year-old girl rushing from his room. In the ceiling was a large hole. The child's mother had let her down on a rope to rifle his baggage.

In spite of danger and inconvenience, the clergyman saw more of the country than most of his predecessors. His account of the land, the people, and the antiquities stands as one of the most reliable. Methodically, he drew plans of royal tombs, sketched monuments, and accurately described others. He observed that the Sphinx had been cut from solid rock, not constructed; and he guessed, correctly, that the receptacles found in tombs—later called canopic jars—contained the viscera of mummies. Pococke was one of the first writers to denounce the destruction he saw all around him.

He and other early travelers left us magnificent drawings and descriptions of monuments, as well as fascinating insights into village life. But ancient Egypt still wore its veil of mystery. No one understood its past or how to read its forgotten language.

In May 1798, Napoleon Bonaparte embarked from the French port of Toulon with an expeditionary force of 38,000 men for the conquest of Egypt. He hoped to expand the territory of France while limiting the power

of England in the East. The result of his military adventure would be the opening up of Egypt's wonders to the West. The French expedition can rightly be called the beginning of modern Egyptology.

With the army and the navy, the general brought a corps of scholars—more than a hundred men schooled in every discipline. He offered them the opportunity to study Egypt and record their observations for the rest of the world. With enthusiasm, the specialists set to work: Artists sketched the antiquities, engineers studied irrigation methods, mapmakers set down the topography of Egypt. Often the work was carried out in the face of hardship and danger.

Vivant Denon, a skillful young artist, risked death or capture to follow an army detachment as it marched south. Sketching furiously, engrossed in his task, Denon was often left alone among picturesque ruins, unaware that the soldiers had moved on. Then, in January 1799, Denon with his military escort rounded a bend of the Nile and saw the temples of Luxor and Karnak. We are told that the troops halted and burst into applause at the sight. "Without an order being given, the men formed their ranks and presented arms, to the accompaniment of the drums and the bands," wrote an army lieutenant.

Besides his select group of intellectuals, dubbed by the military "the donkeys," Napoleon brought with him the first printing press seen in Egypt. Works could now be published quickly and cheaply in Arabic, French, and Greek. He also founded the French Institute in Cairo, a research facility that still exists. In due course, the 24-volume *Description de l'Égypte* appeared. An encyclopedic record of the nation's antiquities, natural history, and contemporary customs, it thrust Egypt into the center of the world stage. Beautifully illustrated folios provided source material for European artists, who painted charmingly realistic scenes of

Egyptian life without ever leaving home. The *Description* contains valuable information on the crumbling monuments, including some that no longer exist.

Crucial to a real understanding of ancient Egypt were the mysterious inscriptions. French soldiers digging fortifications near the town of Rosetta found the key—a bilingual inscription in Greek, which could be read, and Egyptian, which could not. The story of the Rosetta Stone and its decipherment unfolds in a later chapter of this book.

With the coming of the French, Egypt was no longer protected by its remoteness or the difficulties of travel. The 19th century was to be the great period of European exploration and plunder. Most foreign agents were obsessed with acquisition, either for their own national museums or for anyone willing to pay. A competition began for the largest, the most unusual, and the best examples of Egyptian artifacts.

Mohammed Ali, pasha of Egypt after the departure of the French, wished to bring his country into the modern world, and he saw the advantage of using European expertise. If some of these same Europeans showed an interest in hauling off antiquities, he made no objection. Surely there was plenty for everyone; what difference could it possibly make if these foreigners took away a few statues and sarcophagi? Under Mohammed Ali, men such as Giovanni Belzoni, Henry Salt, and Bernardino Drovetti scoured the country for anything ancient and movable. Their enterprise enriched the collections of the British Museum, the Louvre, and the Egyptian Museum in Turin.

Of all those who shared in this wholesale sack of Egypt, Belzoni stands out as the most flamboyant. Italian by birth, English by adoption, he once worked as a sideshow strong man in London. At Sadler's Wells Theatre, where he carried a pyramid of men on his shoulders, he was advertised on the playbill as the "Patagonian Sampson." It was not his great strength

that took him to Egypt, but rather his inventive mind and rich imagination.

Belzoni arrived in Cairo in 1815 and offered to build the pasha a pumping machine that would efficiently move water for irrigation. Nothing came of his ambitions to improve Egyptian agriculture, but he quickly saw the possibilities in collecting antiquities. For the next four years he succeeded brilliantly, overcoming every obstacle. Agents of Drovetti, his rival, threatened to cut his throat if he continued collecting; armed Arabs attacked him; workmen refused to work, but he cajoled, badgered, and bribed them into doing the job.

In 1817 Belzoni journeyed up the Nile to Abu Simbel to uncover the temple that lay behind the gigantic statues of Ramses II. Digging alongside his workmen, he cleared away centuries of drifted sand. Light penetrated the pillared hall inside, revealing "one of the most magnificent of temples, enriched with beautiful intaglios, painting, colossal figures." The monument became so well known that it was saved by international effort in the 1960's when water rising behind the Aswan High Dam threatened to engulf it.

In the Valley of the Kings, Belzoni opened several tombs. Faced with a blocked passage, he fashioned a battering ram and smashed through, obliterating seal impressions and objects behind the door. In other tombs elsewhere the destruction went on: "I sought a resting-place, found one, and contrived to sit; but when my weight bore on the body of an Egyptian, it crushed it like a band-box. . . . I sunk altogether among the broken mummies, with a crash of bones, rags, and wooden cases, which raised such a dust as kept me motionless for a quarter of an hour. . . . every step I took I crushed a mummy in some part or other."

In 1817 Belzoni found the tomb of Seti I, who died about 1300 B.C. Down in the burial chamber stood the sarcophagus, carved from a single block of translucent alabaster and decorated with tiny inlaid figures. Here was a treasure; nothing like it had been seen before. But the tomb had been plundered—gone were the

Theirs was a legacy of giant strides

A trio of great archeologists helped bring ancient Egypt back to life. Gaston Maspero reclines on the rocks at the site where a colleague recovered some 40 royal mummies once buried in the Valley of the Kings. The Egyptian guide holding the rope, Mohammed Abd er-Rasul, received a £500 reward for revealing the resting place of the kings and queens. The meticulous excavator Flinders Petrie is shown in his later years examining pottery finds. Petrie often criticized the sloppy fieldwork of Auguste Mariette, pictured below with Fifth-Dynasty statues from Saqqara. Mariette made spectacular discoveries but kept incomplete records. His excavations at Saqqara, where he found mummified bulls in 60-ton granite sarcophagi, made him famous. **Overleaf:** Swarming over the hillside north of Queen Hatshepsut's funerary temple, diggers and basketboys—the unsung heroes of Egyptology—labor to clear a ravine outside the temple wall. Honeycombed with the tombs of nobles and priests, the area was explored by Herbert Winlock, who in 1929 found there the tomb of 18th-Dynasty Queen Merytamun, the coffin stripped by thieves.

mummy and almost everything else that was movable.

The mummy's fate is part of the long story of tomb robbery in Egypt. As early as the Fourth Dynasty in the reign of Cheops, builder of the Great Pyramid, there is evidence of pillage. Curses inscribed on early tombs threaten with vengeance those who inflict damage, and promise blessings to those who care for the tomb. With the fall of the Old Kingdom an epidemic of looting began. The starving people traded the tomb treasures for bread.

The Middle Kingdom brought better days, and the tombs flourished as before. Only with the lean years of Dynasty 20 did robbery become prevalent again, this time with the connivance of government officials. A surviving papyrus tells the story: The mayor of East Thebes charged the mayor of West Thebes, who policed the cemeteries, with neglecting his duties and helping the thieves. A commission sent to investigate found nine royal tombs intact, only one violated. But there was room for suspicion—the commission probably avoided the violated burials! Accusations continued to fly, and tombs continued to be plundered. As a last resort, the priests collected all the surviving royal mummies and hid them in a safer place, where they remained undisturbed for 3,000 years.

In 1871 a goatherd and part-time tomb robber, Ahmed Abd er-Rasul, found the cache of mummies while searching for a lost kid near the temple of Hatshepsut at Deir el Bahri. Ahmed came from the village of Qurna, whose inhabitants had been robbing tombs in the hillside west of Thebes for centuries. Often they lived in the tombs among the "hands, feet, or sculls" strewn around the dark caves. Belzoni had made friends with them and bought their antiquities; Napoleon's men had been greeted with volleys of stones.

When Ahmed found the royal mummies, he was cautious. He entered the tomb only a few times in ten years and took into his confidence only family members. Gradually, papyri, scarabs, and canopic jars began to appear on the market. By this time, the Egyptian

government had set up an organization to protect antiquities. The Director-General, Gaston Maspero, suspected that a royal tomb had been found. Some clever detective work led him and Egyptologist Emil Brugsch to the guilty family; two of the brothers were arrested, thrown on the ground, and beaten with palm rods on the soles of their feet. They refused to confess. Later, Ahmed's eldest brother Mohammed, fearing for his own safety, led authorities to the treasure.

Brugsch entered the grave deep inside the cliffs of the Theban necropolis. By flickering candlelight he beheld the mortal remains of such illustrious pharaohs as Ramses II, Thutmose III, and Seti I—Belzoni's missing mummy. "I still wonder if I am not dreaming when I see and touch what were the bodies of so many famous personages," Maspero was to write later. The buried kings were removed and sent north by boat. Along the Nile, crowds gathered for the funeral procession—the women wailing, the men shooting off shotguns. They mourned as much for the defeat of their friends, the tomb robbers, as they did for the dead pharaohs.

With the work of scholars like Maspero, Egyptology made rapid progress. Besides supervising the mummy project, Maspero went "fishing for statues" in the Temple of Amun-Re at Karnak. Rising groundwater had drowned a rich mine of objects buried by priests in antiquity. Using oil cans for pails, workmen bailed, then groped in the mud with bare hands. "Seven hundred stone monuments have already come out of the water," Maspero wrote, "Pharaohs enthroned, queens standing upright, priests of Amun . . . indeed, a whole population returns to the upper air."

Maspero followed in the footsteps of another French archeologist, Auguste Mariette. The latter had been appointed the first conservator of ancient monuments, a position he used to protect antiquities from vandals and thieves. Careless tourists enraged him, especially one American visitor who toured Upper Egypt in 1870

19

"I was struck dumb with amazement"

Howard Carter peered through a chink in Tutankhamun's tomb. "At first I could see nothing," he said. Then details within emerged: "strange animals, statues, and gold—everywhere the glint of gold." Lord Carnarvon asked, "Can you see anything?" Carter replied, "Yes, wonderful things." And this was only the beginning—four rooms were heaped up with treasure. The mummy lay encased in solid gold, one of three nested coffins (left). When the news broke, visitors and journalists swarmed around the tomb, impeding work. Carter had erected a steel door, and armed guards escorted workmen, shown here bearing part of a couch and a bust of the king that seems to walk by itself. It took Carter and a staff of experts ten years to clear the tomb.

"with a pot of tar in one hand and a brush in the other, leaving on all the temples the indelible and truly disgraceful record of his passage." To Mariette goes the credit for establishing an Egyptian national museum that would protect antiquities and keep them in Egypt.

Many other scholars brought special talents to the growing discipline. A pioneering English archeologist, William Matthew Flinders Petrie, was shocked by the wastefulness of early excavators who concentrated on showy objects and ignored such run-of-the-mill items as potsherds and mud walls. Petrie believed these "trifles" to be important. By applying step-by-step methodology, he transformed a treasure hunt into a science. "Most people think of excavating as a pleasing sort of holiday amusement," he wrote, "but it takes about as much care and management as any other business."

Petrie's spartan life-style became legendary. While other diggers ate elegant food on plush houseboats, he was content to live in a tomb or a mud hut and eat out of tin cans. "He has a cot bed in the tomb of Nefermaat," a visitor wrote, "a few . . . books . . . and two tents, one a kitchen with a petroleum stove." He was his own photographer, copyist, and chemist. Though his students abhorred the rigorous life in camp, they revered Petrie as a great archeologist.

In the 20th century, German, French, and English archeologists were joined by the Americans. Excavations enriched the museums of New York and Boston, until today their collections are among the finest in the world. James Henry Breasted of the University of Chicago led an intensive campaign to copy monument inscriptions before they were lost to decay or vandalism.

The scientists of this period were occupied with more than just a re-examination of known sites. In 1907 a dedicated archeologist began an association with an English nobleman that would have stunning consequences for Egyptology. In that year, the Fifth Earl of Carnarvon, having decided to do some excavating, hired Howard Carter to direct the project. Carter had worked with Petrie and other scholars. A gifted artist,

he had copied temple carvings at Deir el Bahri. The Egyptian government had appointed him an inspector of monuments.

Theodore Davis, a rich American, relinquished his rights to dig in the Valley of the Kings in 1914. Almost everyone believed the valley to be exhausted, but Carter disagreed. With Lord Carnarvon's financial backing, he took up the concession. Their efforts were interrupted by World War I, and even Carnarvon had become discouraged. Carter pleaded for one more season to pursue the goal that had become his obsession— the tomb of Tutankhamun. He knew that Davis had found some Tutankhamun artifacts. The tomb itself had never been discovered because it was concealed by the rubble quarried out of a larger tomb just above it. Even the ancient robbers had been fooled; except for an abortive break-in, probably soon after Tutankhamun's funeral, the tomb remained intact until our own time.

Like Heinrich Schliemann, who discovered the site of ancient Troy, Carter found exactly what he believed to be there. In November 1922, his workmen uncovered a staircase. As they cleared it, a doorway came into view, affixed with royal seals showing the jackal symbol of the god Anubis above nine defeated captives. "It was a thrilling moment," Carter wrote. "Literally anything might lie beyond that passage, and it needed all my self-control to keep from breaking down the doorway, and investigating then and there."

But for nearly three agonizing weeks he waited for the arrival of Lord Carnarvon from London. Then the clearing continued. Finally, on November 26, 1922, they entered the tomb, where the glitter of gold and the sight of beautiful things made the onlookers "strangely silent and subdued." Carter's reward was spectacular. "King Tut" became a household phrase. The press carried daily bulletins from the Valley of the Kings as work progressed. Today the wealth of Tutankhamun's tomb fills gallery after gallery in Cairo's Egyptian Museum. Some of these treasures appear in the portfolio that follows, and elsewhere in this book.

Spectacular finds come along once in a lifetime, but there are always perplexing riddles to tease the imagination. New scientific tools help solve them. An intriguing example is the recent identification of Queen Tiy. Eighty years ago a female mummy with wavy brown hair and no identifying marks turned up in the tomb of Amunhotep II. She was called simply "Elder Lady." In 1975 scientists X-rayed the mummy's head and discovered that the facial contours resembled those of Queen Thuya, mother of Tiy. With the maternal link suggested, electrons were used to "fingerprint" the minerals in Elder Lady's hair and in a known lock of Queen Tiy's hair—found in Tutankhamun's tomb. The results positively identified the mummy as Queen Tiy, wife of Amunhotep III and possibly the grandmother of Tutankhamun.

New discoveries are coming out of Egypt. I was fortunate to participate in the ongoing excavation of the Mut Temple complex at Karnak, a part of the Brooklyn Museum Theban Expedition in Egypt. Two Englishwomen dug there in the 1890's, but archeologists have all but ignored the site. The Karnak temples honor the Theban gods Amun, his consort, Mut, and their son, Khonsu. An avenue lined with sphinxes, connecting Mut's temple with Amun's, may have been built by Tutankhamun. Nearly surrounded by a lake symbolizing the water from which all life came, the Mut Temple is the centerpiece of a 25-acre complex. We uncovered foundations of walls and colonnades, potsherds, and sculpture—the puzzle pieces of Egyptian history. But it may take years to understand the temple's intriguing story.

Most people believe the sands of Egypt have yielded all the secrets of the past. Nothing could be further from the truth. So much lies buried that it will take generations of digging even to begin to fill the gaps in our knowledge. The search goes on for clues to the civilization that has already given us, as Herodotus said, "such a number of works which defy description."

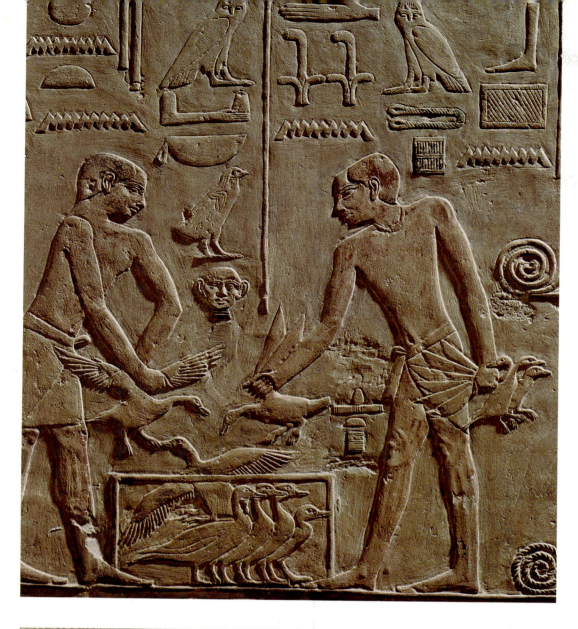

"And small birds they eat also"

Egypt lies on a major migratory route for water birds shuttling between Europe and central and southern Africa. Twice each year great throngs pause on Nile marshes and lakes, resting after flights across the Mediterranean or the Sahara's wastes. In predynastic days incredible numbers—along with local wildfowl—gave Egyptians such a handy supply there was little incentive for domesticating flocks.

Old Kingdom tomb paintings show teams of men with huge nets hauling in catches. Clap traps and snares also took birds. Those captured went to the table or to fattening pens. Fluttering geese (top) and pigeons and ducks (opposite) on wall reliefs dating from about 2400 B.C. are so detailed that sometimes we can even identify the species. Like the crane at left, the fowl might be force-fattened with food crammed down their throats.

The birds' flesh was eaten roasted or boiled. Organs and extracts went into medicines—papyri give prescriptions: goose-fat potions "to treat the belly" or salves "to keep flies from biting."

Birds figured in sacrifices to the gods; Ramses II alone offered 360,000 during a 31-year period. Geese were sacred to the Nile god, yet still were eaten—a contradiction which perplexed Herodotus. He also noted that Egyptians ate small birds uncooked, "merely first salting" (pickling) them.

61

"He who tends his crop will eat it"

Cultivation of grains in Egypt traces its beginnings far back beyond the dawn of recorded time. Barley husks have been found in the intestines of predynastic mummies. Kernels of wheat have turned up in Stone Age storage pits dug in the desert's edge and lined with basketry. Egypt's land was superbly suited to such crops, and the nation became an envied granary. It was a breadbasket of the Roman Empire.

Tomb paintings give precise details of how the grain was grown. After seed was scattered over the Nile mud, sheep driven across the field trampled the grain into the ground. When the crop ripened, inspectors came with measuring lines (bottom) to set the government's quota; wheat was heavily taxed through all antiquity. Farmers seeking to curry the officials' favor offered refreshments and gifts. Then men with sickles lopped off the grain heads and hauled them in baskets and nets to the threshing floor (middle). Laborers might catnap or play a flute for a restful moment; girl gleaners might fall into a hair-pulling spat over territorial encroachments.

Oxen or donkeys, prodded by shouts and sticks, threshed the grain; men with wooden pitchforks (top) kept adding the heads underfoot from stacks around the floor. Then winnowers, their hair shielded from the dust by linen cloths, tossed the grain with wooden scoops to separate kernel from chaff. Samples of the cleaned grain went to the master for inspection, the rest to tallying and the granary.

"Supply my needs of bread and beer"

Staple foods of the poor, the rich, and the gods, bread and beer played such a fundamental role that in Ramesside times the words even became an occasional phrase used like our "hello." Preserved loaves and jars with beer residues have been found at predynastic sites.

In a model from the tomb of Meketre (top), scribes seated in a courtyard record measures of grain being brought from the threshing floor. Laborers carry sacks up stairs and empty them into granary bins. To make flour, the grain was pounded with mortar and pestle or ground with a roller on flat stones. Dough in big batches for a great household might be kneaded with the feet instead of by hand. Loaves were baked inside an oval oven; flat bread was cooked by putting dough on the outside, or on flat hearths such as those used today.

Barley and bread grains, worked into a mash in earthen jars (left), fermented to become the drink that neither the living nor the dead could do without.

"I made vineyards without limit"

Ramses III might have been exaggerating a bit, but it's a safe bet he needed extensive arbors to supply his demands for wine. His accounts show that he gave 20,078 jars as offerings to the god Amun, and contributed 39,510 more for use at temple rites. Then, of course, there were the requirements for palace feasting.

Beer was brewed almost daily in the average household, but wine, because of the time and care involved in its making, was a costly drink enjoyed mostly by the rich. Royal tombs from the earliest dynasties held caches of jars, and wall reliefs and paintings in burials of later nobles show wine making—and drinking.

Vines grew best in northern Egypt, particularly in the Delta region. They yielded grapes for half a dozen kinds of wine, though it's hard to tell from names the Egyptians used how they equate with modern types. Red wines seem to have been favored in early periods, whites in later dynasties. Most vineyards lay within walls of estates, with the plants trained to trellises; gardeners watered them from earthen jugs and shooed away birds with slingshots and shouts.

At harvest time, pickers carried the bunches of grapes to crushing vats, where barefoot workers stomped out the juice. while holding overhead straps for balance. For extra pressing the must went into sacks—twisted and levered with poles. An agile workman might add his bit by bridging the press (top). Juice fermented in open urns; finished wine went into jars. Lumps of clay sealed the reed stoppers.

Markings put on the bottles gave as much information as modern labels—often more. They bore the name of the estate, its location, the vineyard, the name of the vintner, the date, and an assessment of the quality—"good," "twice good," "three times good," "genuine," "sweet." One from an Amarna tomb was downgraded as "for merrymaking." Gourmets note: 1344 B.C. rated a great vintage year.

They labor on the river

In a simple one-man skiff made by tying together bundles of papyrus reeds, a fisherman poises a club for the catfish he has caught on a hand line. Behind him, balanced on the stern of a larger boat fashioned in the same way, a seaman poles his craft through the crowded waters.

Egyptians ate fish from early times; hooks made of shell and ivory, bone harpoons, and fish remains have been unearthed in prehistoric middens. Ebbing Nile floods left fishes stranded in low spots, easy to gather when the waters receded. Tomb inscriptions tell of that bounty. The reliefs also record the sculptors' concern with accuracy—we can identify some 24 present-day species of Nile fish in various wall carvings.

Light, easily paddled papyrus craft had shallow drafts well suited to the marshes and channels of the Nile. No one knows when man first learned to sail, but the earliest record of ships and shipbuilding occurs in Egyptian drawings. Large papyrus boats developed logically from bundled rafts in a land where wood was scarce. The trees, mostly scrubby acacias, yielded planks only a few feet long. As wooden ships evolved there, they were made of short boards lashed together much the way reed bundles were. The tradition stuck; millenniums later Herodotus likened Egyptian shipbuilders to bricklayers. But by 2500 B.C. Egypt's craft could barge great stones down the Nile for the pyramids, her traders could ply the Mediterranean, her shipyards could turn out a 100-foot boat in 17 days.

High sterns helped the crews push their craft off sandbars. Awnings served as cabins, and cargo was stowed on deck. Bipod masts—slim, twin poles tied at the peak—developed because only the gunwales of reed boats could support spars. On big boats rowers stood to dip oars, stroked by plopping backwards onto benches—oarsmen's kilts had seat pads sewn on. Even figureheads had unusual touches, facing aft instead of forward.

Ships slowly changed from these Old Kingdom beginnings, but Egypt remained a land for those who labored on the river.

Overleaf: Strata and sail on a tired Nile

Beneath stark cliffs near Beni Hasan the Nile sweeps by, "weary of endlessly murmuring . . . that it has traveled too far." Broad-bottomed, cargo-carrying naggars and slim feluccas coursing the river argue that here still lives the age of sail.

Pyramids: Building for Eternity

I.E.S. Edwards

May you cause to be enduring
this pyramid . . .
for ever and ever
                    Pyramid Texts

The ancient Greeks numbered them among the Seven Wonders of the World. Early Christian tradition identified them as Joseph's granaries, built, according to the Book of Genesis, in preparation for the seven years of famine. Arab historians linked them with the Biblical flood, suggesting that the written wisdom of mankind, or even the human race, found refuge in the imperishable pyramids of Egypt.

Today we count some 80 major and minor pyramids dotting the west bank of the Nile, most of them in the 55-mile stretch between Abu Roash and the Faiyum. In my four decades as an Egyptologist I have visited many of them, sometimes crawling like a snake through dark corridors choked with the rubble of centuries. I have clambered up a heap of stones to get a handhold on the entrance to a pyramid—and found myself clinging helplessly to the ledge when the heap collapsed under my feet. I have walked in chambers and passageways where the rock all around me was so decayed that the slightest touch brought down a shower of loose stone upon my head.

Today most of the rubble has been cleared, and most of the pyramids have been explored, studied, and documented. We know they are tombs, yet still they fire our imagination. Some say that such colossal structures could not have been built with the simple tools of ancient Egypt; the builders must have levitated the huge stones into place by magic, or watched in awe as

"There was constructed for me a pyramidal tomb out of stone"

A phrase from the "Story of Sinuhe" recalls the Pyramid Age. Such words might have been spoken by Djoser; his Step Pyramid was the first tomb in Egypt built entirely of stone. Restored buildings stand amid the rubble of others as if expecting their monarch's return. And so does his pyramid; through 46 centuries it has awaited his tread on its magical stairway to the stars.

visitors from outer space lent skills that our scientists have yet to discover. Others see in the myriad measurements of the Great Pyramid of Cheops at Giza a key to events past, present, and future. And some recent writers claim to have detected a mysterious force in the pyramidal shape itself. Inside even a table-top pyramid of cardboard, they say, a razor blade keeps its edge, and fruit and milk stay fresh.

But to Egyptologists, there are no "mysteries" about these great structures, only questions we cannot yet answer. For example, we do not know with certainty how the pyramids were built. But we do know something about ancient Egyptian building methods. What seems the most probable method for the pyramids unfolds in the paintings at the end of this chapter.

Using techniques that were known to the ancient Egyptians, we might duplicate the pyramids today. Our chief problem would probably be the mustering of a work force large enough to undertake such a project. But the Egyptians had little trouble assembling the necessary manpower. Farm workers by the tens of thousands had to be idle for three or four months of the year, due to the inundation of the Nile. Food was cheap, the labor force was enormous, and the efficient Egyptians knew how to mobilize both.

There is another question that is seldom asked, and to me it is a more intriguing one: Why? For what reasons did the ancient kings choose to be buried in tombs of pyramidal form? To understand the answer, we must remember that a pyramid is an expression of evolving religious ideas. In its purest form it is, almost literally, a sunburst turned to stone.

Before we consider the purpose of this design, we should look at what preceded it. For new ideas did not usually sweep away older notions; they were simply superimposed. Some elements persisted long after their purpose was forgotten.

One concept that never changed throughout Egyptian history was the need to preserve the dead body from decay so that the spirit of its owner could re-enter

"Is there another like Imhotep?"

It was well-earned praise, this passage from a New Kingdom text. By 600 B.C., Imhotep—architect and chief minister of King Djoser—had become a demigod. His devotees offered countless images like the bronze statuette below. Greece and Rome saw in him their god of healing until Christianity swept him away. Time all but swept away the great wall that stretched more than a mile around Imhotep's masterwork, the Step Pyramid complex at Saqqara. A restored section of the wall (opposite) suggests the grandeur of this monument for Djoser, whose limestone image once gazed with crystal eyes from a cell at his pyramid's foot.

it at will. In the Predynastic Era, before about 3100 B.C., and later in the case of all but the elite, bodies were placed in shallow graves in the desert, where preservation occurred naturally by the desiccating action of the warm, dry sand. Such graves were covered with low mounds of sand and gravel—and were soon eroded to oblivion by the desert wind. By the end of the Predynastic Era, more substantial mounds of sunbaked brick and rubble were built. These gave better protection from the ravages of jackals and marked the grave more clearly for relatives bringing offerings. But burial at greater depth prevented natural desiccation. Thus, in time, the art of mummification was invented.

Survival after death was too important to entrust to body preservation alone. And so an effigy of stone, wood, or other durable material became accepted as a "second body," especially when inscribed with the owner's name. I believe that this idea, more than any other factor, led to the rise of the art of sculpture.

Funerary customs, whatever their nature, needed magic to make them effective. Magic could be imitative: Make an image of something, then endow it with reality by magical rites. The size of an image did not matter, nor whether it was freestanding, carved in relief, or simply painted on a wall. Actual boats buried near the pyramids of Giza were intended to bear their owners upon the waters of the next world, but for a queen of about three centuries later, wooden models were considered enough.

Spells were another form of magic. Hundreds of them were uttered by priests from predynastic times until long after the Giza pyramids were built. The whole repertoire would have been lost had they not been inscribed on the walls inside the pyramids of the Fifth-Dynasty ruler Unas and his immediate successors. Known as the Pyramid Texts, they often referred to conditions long outmoded. "Throw off the sand from your face!" one of them tells a king buried in a pyramid. No identifiable predynastic royal tombs have been found, but such spells—though transcribed cen-

"As though heaven were within it"

The New Kingdom visitor rhapsodized over the little temple at the Old Kingdom Pyramid of Meidum (opposite). There was more within the pyramid than he knew: a seven-stepped monument inside an eight-stepped structure inside a true pyramid's sloping triangles. Shorn of its smooth facades by generations of stone-hungry builders, the towerlike ruin shows portions of its two stepped phases (bottom diagram). The base of the pyramid that may have soared 300 feet above the desert now lies buried under a circlet of sand. When—and if—it was completed, it may have been the first true pyramid in the world. The Bent Pyramid, begun earlier, could have been the first, but halfway up the builders blunted it to a rhomboid (third diagram).

There may be more within the Meidum ruin than *we* know. Perhaps it began as a mastaba, the tomb whose basic design (top diagram) outlasted the Pyramid Age. The Step Pyramid at Saqqara (second diagram) began with a structure that suggests a mound, a throwback to burials before the dynasties began.

turies later—show that the early kings were buried, like ordinary people, right in the desert sand.

The tombs of nearly all the kings of the First and Second Dynasties have come to light at Abydos; possibly some of these kings also had mastaba-tombs at Saqqara. "Mastaba" is a modern Arabic word for the low bench outside many an Egyptian door; there the man of the house likes to take his ease and sip coffee with his friends. Like the bench, the ancient mastaba was a boxlike structure. Its outer walls, in early examples, resembled the walls of a royal palace, with simulated doorways recessed between towerlike projections. Inside, it was divided by brick walls into cells containing funerary equipment. Beneath it was a pit hewn in the rock; this too was divided into compartments, the central one being the burial chamber. And over the pit rose a low rectangular mound of sand cased with brick, hidden from view by the superstructure.

The brick-covered mound had no structural function. In fact, its sloping sides were a source of weakness. The tomb-builders probably realized this, for in later First Dynasty mastabas they built brick mounds with stepped sides. But why include a mound at all?

It is not difficult to recognize in the mound a survival of the sand-and-rubble mound of a predynastic grave. The ancient Egyptians were always reluctant to discard anything once it had become a part of the funerary paraphernalia. But in this case there may also have been a more esoteric reason. Each year, the Egyptians saw patches of high ground appear from the waters of the Nile as the flood began to recede; from this sprang the belief that the world began as a mound rising from the waters of chaos. So, the mound of the predynastic tomb could have been regarded as a replica of the primeval mound, the source of all life, and by imitative magic its life-giving powers would have been imparted to the person buried beneath it.

Apparently there was no radical difference in the first two dynasties between the tombs of kings and those of the nobility. The divergence came at the begin-

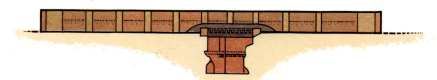

First Dynasty: Mastaba resembles a palace, though rooms lack doors. Sand mound covers burial pit. Middle chamber is for the body.

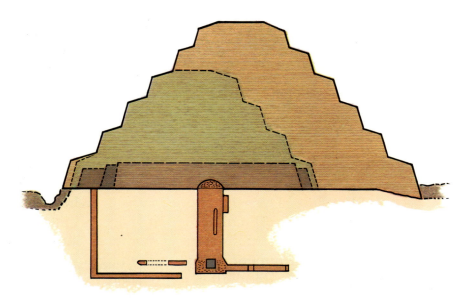

Third Dynasty: Djoser's men hewed deep burial chamber, enlarged its superstructure several times to create Step Pyramid.

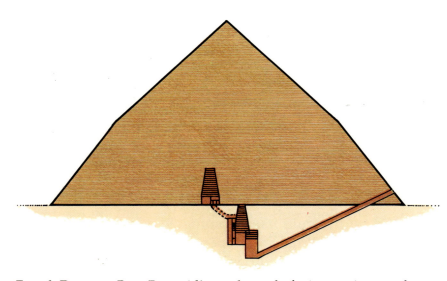

Fourth Dynasty: Bent Pyramid's northern shaft aims at circumpolar stars. Western shaft (not shown) leads to upper chamber.

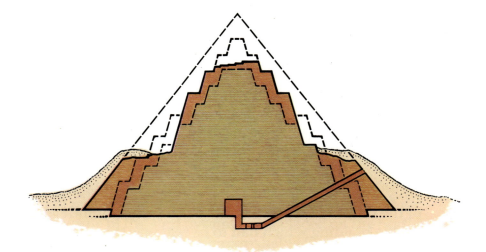

Fourth Dynasty: Snefru achieves true pyramid at Meidum. Dashed lines show its stages, shaded areas its remains. Diagrams look west.

"Cheops is one belonging to the horizon"

So he named his pyramid—and so it perpetuates his name as it dominates the desert horizon. Largest of the group at Giza, the Great Pyramid of Cheops contains 2.3 million stone blocks, some weighing up to 15 tons. Here Chephren's, in the center, appears taller because it stands on higher ground, though each dwarfs the tomb of Mycerinus and its three subsidiary pyramids. The peak of Chephren's pyramid (above) still retains remnants of its original casing of fine, dressed limestone.

The major pyramids of the Fourth Dynasty at Dahshur and Giza are still largely intact—though stripped of most of their outer casings—so that we cannot be sure of the pattern of their internal construction. But the less well-preserved subsidiary pyramids at Giza show that a true pyramid does indeed mask an inner step pyramid. Another feature retained from the step pyramid was the sloping entrance corridor with a horizontal continuation, running from the northern side to the burial chamber. And in several true pyramids a small chapel stood at the entrance, probably a relic of the temple located in that position in the step pyramids.

No sooner had the true pyramid evolved under Snefru than it reached its zenith under his son and successor, Khufu, who began his reign about 2570 B.C. Khufu is better known to us by his Greek name, Cheops, and remembered as the builder of a pyramid that was never surpassed either in size or in architectural perfection: the Great Pyramid of Giza.

Profiting from the practical experience gained at Dahshur and Meidum, the builders of the Great Pyramid erected a massive monument whose base covers 13.1 acres. When complete, it rose to a height of 481.4 feet; today the top 31 feet are missing. Skilled masons and stonecutters fitted its casing stones to each other with clearances of hundredths of an inch. And the difference between its longest and shortest sides was less than eight inches, on lengths of more than 750 feet.

The accuracy of the squareness of its base seems all the more remarkable when we remember that an outcrop of rock, which was left unleveled in the middle of

Theirs was the greatness of Giza

From the sands around the pyramids of
Giza have come images of the kings who
raised these tombs. Ironies of fate link
the images and their namesakes' mighty
monuments. A tiny ivory figurine about
three inches tall (above) survives as
the only known statue of Cheops, builder
of the greatest pyramid of all.
Chephren's tomb stands second to Cheops's,
yet his life-size image in diorite (left)
ranks first in artistic merit among Old
Kingdom statuary. It shows the ruler on
a lion-legged throne adorned with the
lotus and papyrus of the two Egypts.
A falcon symbolizes the king as the living
god Horus—and perhaps braces a weak point
in the statue's construction as well.

   In a triad (opposite) from his temple,
Mycerinus appears less formal and aloof
than his predecessors. He strides between
the cow-horned goddess Hathor and the
chief deity of the seventh nome, or province.
Many such triads, each with a different
nome god, may have lined the temple to affirm
the king's dominance over all of Egypt.

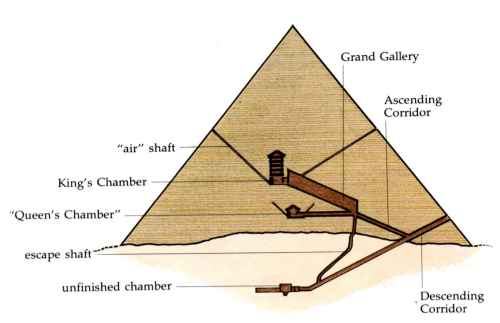

Grand Gallery

Ascending Corridor

"air" shaft

King's Chamber

"Queen's Chamber"

escape shaft

unfinished chamber

Descending Corridor

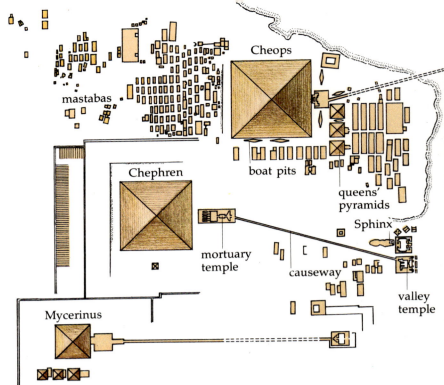

Cheops

mastabas

boat pits

queens' pyramids

Chephren

Sphinx

mortuary temple

causeway

valley temple

Mycerinus

The Grand Gallery: wonder within a wonder

No other Old Kingdom monument has a chamber to compare with the lofty, upsloping passage aptly named the Grand Gallery in the Great Pyramid of Cheops. Above benchlike ramps at each side, polished walls rise seven and a half feet above the steeply pitched floor. Then seven courses of blocks, each offset three inches, rise in a corbeled vault to a ceiling 28 feet above the floor. A modern stair eases a climb that appears level to the camera's eye. Longer than half a football field, this impressive void pierces the pyramid to its heart—the King's Chamber, itself an engineering triumph with its five weight-relieving chambers. Shafts and corridors vein the mighty mass. The Queen's Chamber and a bedrock tomb were never completed. A causeway, temples, mastabas, and two more pyramid complexes lie outside.

the site, would have prevented the ancient engineers from making diagonal checks. Probably this rock was not removed for practical reasons; it reduced the amount of core material needed. But perhaps it was also kept because it constituted a natural central mound, an evocation of one of the oldest and most persistent of Egyptian funerary customs.

The pyramid's four faces were oriented almost precisely toward north, south, east, and west. In order to achieve this, surveyors made sightings on stars in the northern sky. Accuracy was vital—in fact, so important that the sightings would be reenacted in a religious ceremony by the king himself. A Fifth-Dynasty relief shows just such a ceremony, and in a much later text we can read the words that might have been said: "I take the stake and I hold the handle of the mallet. I hold the (measuring) cord. . . ." The royal surveyors knew the king was merely going through the motions, much as a modern dignitary would turn over the first spadeful of earth at a construction project, or lay a cornerstone with a silver trowel.

Externally, the Great Pyramid appears to have been completed without undergoing any significant changes in its original plan. But internally, great changes were made as construction proceeded. From an entrance in the north face, a descending corridor runs in a southward direction, first through the core of

the building and then through the rock bed, for about 345 feet. It then continues horizontally for another 29 feet, where a large chamber was hewed in the rock. A second chamber would probably have been added, but before the first chamber had been finished, the whole plan for an underground burial was abandoned.

Instead, an opening was cut in the ceiling of this descending corridor near the entrance, and from there an upward-sloping corridor was constructed. From its upper end, a level passage leads to what was then intended to be the new burial chamber, a room built of limestone blocks. Today this room is commonly, but incorrectly, called the Queen's Chamber.

But this plan also was abandoned. The ascending corridor was then extended in the form of a magnificent gallery with a corbeled vault, known as the Grand Gallery. It is undoubtedly one of the most remarkable architectural achievements of the Old Kingdom.

At the southern or higher end of the Grand Gallery, a level passage ends in a chamber of red granite called the King's Chamber. In order to reduce direct pressure from the weight of masonry above this chamber, five separate compartments were constructed above its ceiling. Four have flat roofs and the uppermost has a pointed roof. But in spite of these precautions, all nine ceiling blocks of the chamber itself—which together weigh about 400 tons—and some of the roofs of the relieving compartments are now cracked, perhaps as a result of earth tremors. The king's granite sarcophagus, though missing its lid, still lies intact in the chamber, near the west wall. It is an inch wider than the mouth of the ascending corridor and thus could not have been installed after the pyramid was built. It must have been placed in the room as the chamber itself was being constructed.

Kings had long been aware of the need to protect tombs from robbers, and so they took elaborate precautions with their own "houses of eternity." Entrance corridors were usually closed after the burial by heavy portcullises and filled with large blocks of stone. In

Across the Nile, quarrymen hollow a hill

Working away with copper chisels and sledges of wood, stonecutters and hauling crews move countless tons of stone a block at a time. From the quarry wall they cut each block's sides, then crawl over the top to chisel down the back. Wooden wedges, hammered in along the bottom line, split the block free. Later, masons will use copper saws to shape and fit the blocks. Outside, workers drag the rough blocks to waiting boats. One inscribes a stone, another pounds his chisel to sharpen it. A scribe keeps tally. Other workers make bricks by the thousand. No such menial tasks dull the sculptor's senses; with artful strokes he draws a monarch from a stone.

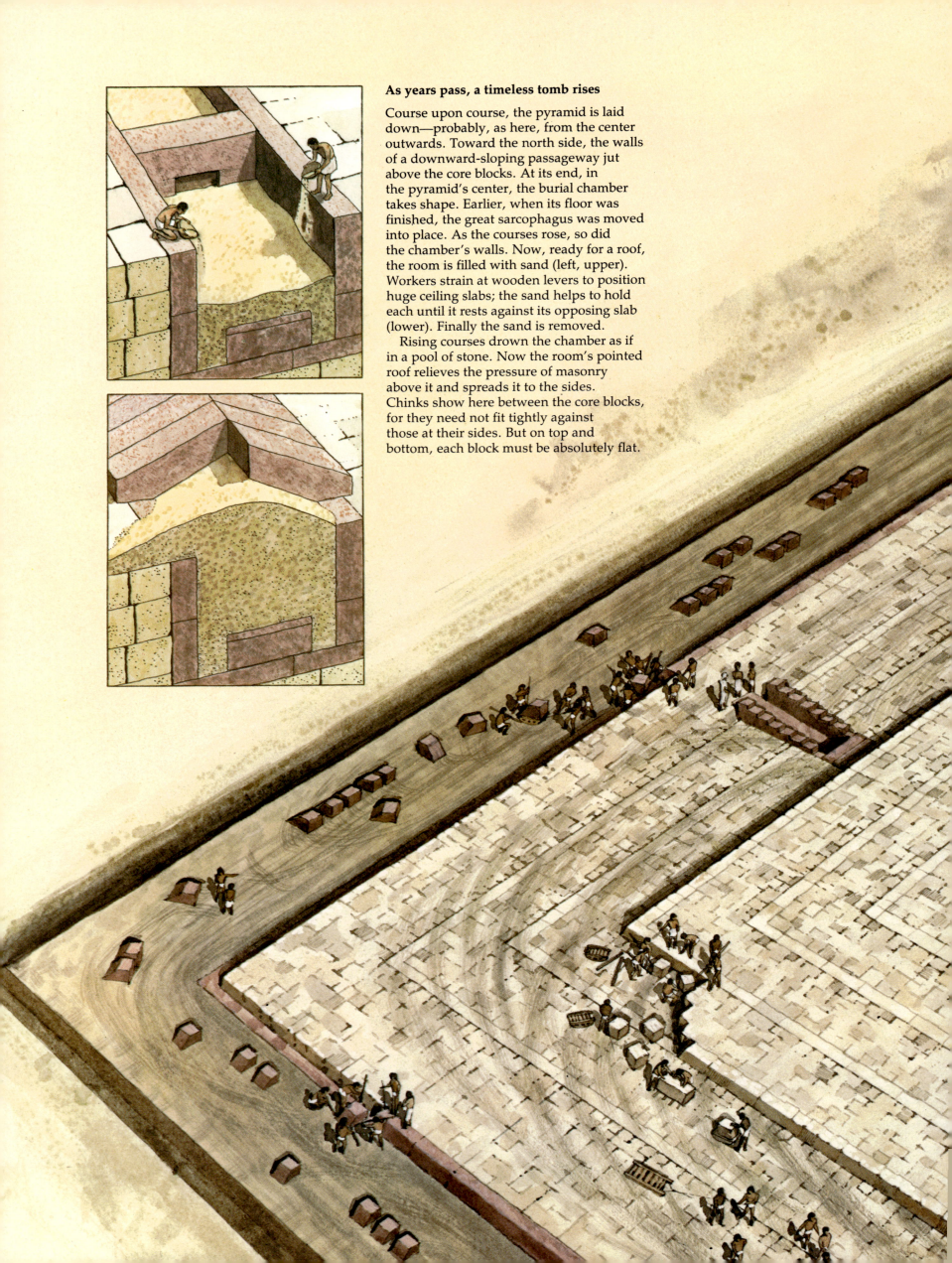

As years pass, a timeless tomb rises

Course upon course, the pyramid is laid down—probably, as here, from the center outwards. Toward the north side, the walls of a downward-sloping passageway jut above the core blocks. At its end, in the pyramid's center, the burial chamber takes shape. Earlier, when its floor was finished, the great sarcophagus was moved into place. As the courses rose, so did the chamber's walls. Now, ready for a roof, the room is filled with sand (left, upper). Workers strain at wooden levers to position huge ceiling slabs; the sand helps to hold each until it rests against its opposing slab (lower). Finally the sand is removed.

Rising courses drown the chamber as if in a pool of stone. Now the room's pointed roof relieves the pressure of masonry above it and spreads it to the sides. Chinks show here between the core blocks, for they need not fit tightly against those at their sides. But on top and bottom, each block must be absolutely flat.

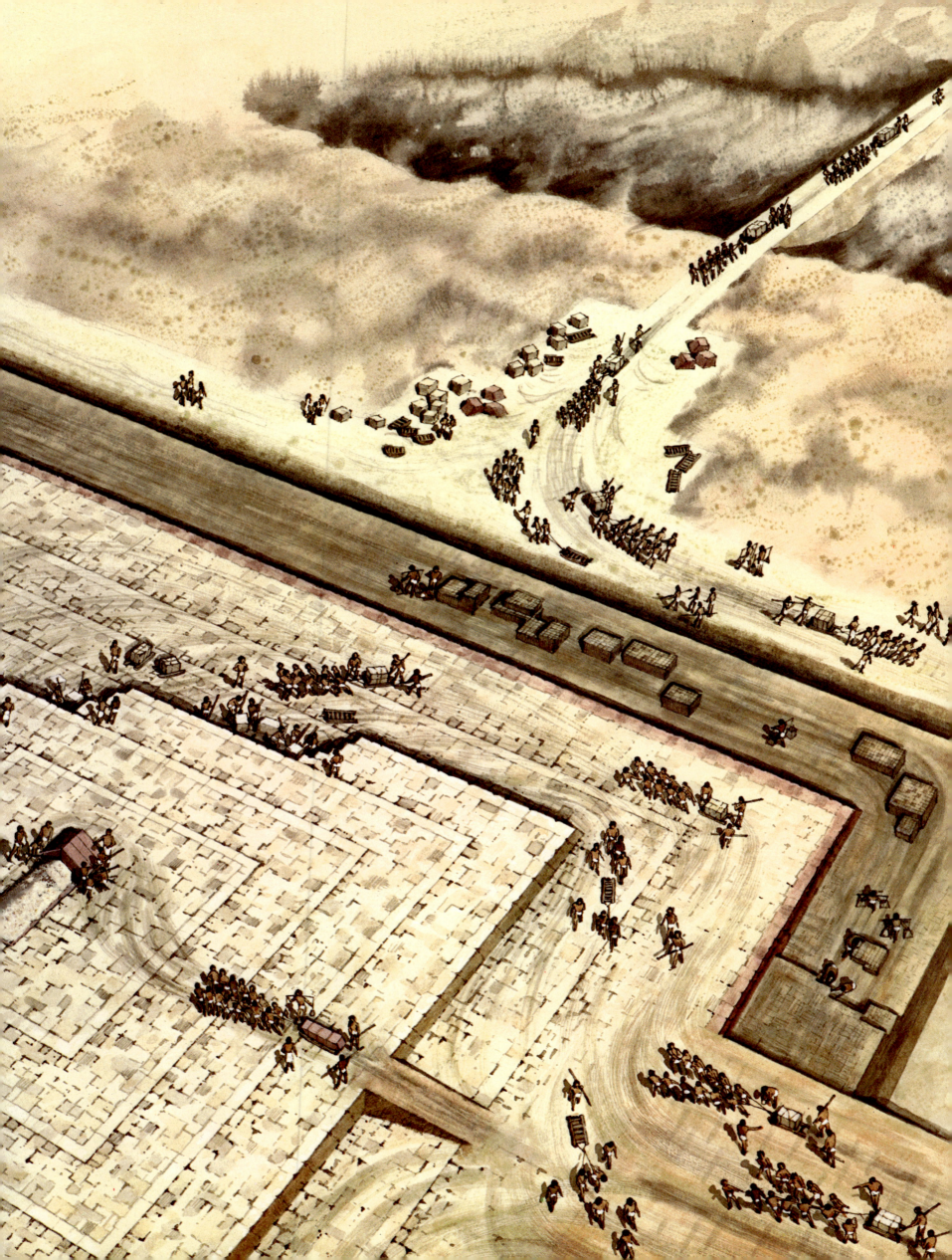

Stones skid skyward on a mountain of bricks

On a massive ramp of sun-baked bricks and rubble, teams haul
the heavy blocks to the rising pyramid. Some laborers carry water
to slick the mud surface; others carry timbers to brake the wooden
sledges lest they slip back when haulers pause. Stonecutters fit
the blocks in a staging area below. Then masons position them above,
aided on outer courses by a brick catwalk that jackets the structure
as pyramid, catwalk, and ramp rise together. A gilded pyramidion
tops off years of work. Months more remain as workers—some
on scaffolds—smooth the slant-faced casing stones. As they work
downward, ramp and catwalk are returned brick by brick to the Nile.

A portable bedroom, fit for a queen

Incredible luck and workmanship that spans 46 centuries show us how a queen slept in the Pyramid Age. Around the bed of Hetepheres, mother of Cheops, curtains hung from a canopy to ensure privacy and provide protection from insects. Gold encased the wooden frame. Tenons and copper sheathing braced its joints, yet it could be easily dismantled. On the jambs gleam the names of the queen's husband, Snefru. The detail above symbolizes his domain— sedge and bee stand for Upper and Lower Egypt, as do vulture and cobra. The box stored curtains. Papyrus blooms adorn the oldest chair in existence. Headrest and sloping bed, typical then, strike one modern scholar as "great for watching TV."

In 1925 a camera tripod struck a patch of plaster near Cheops's Great Pyramid. Under the spot a shaft led down to Hetepheres's tomb, a jumbled mass. Decayed wood had the feel of cigar ash, but gold casings held their shape. For 14 years George Reisner, a master Egyptologist, and his team sifted, recorded, and restored the gilded boudoir for Cairo's Egyptian Museum. The duplicate here appears in Boston's Museum of Fine Arts.

The queen? Gone. Reisner imagined an age-old cover-up: She may have been stolen from an earlier tomb near her husband at Dahshur. Then a terrified bureaucrat got approval for a transfer to the more secure site at Giza—without ever telling Cheops his mother's mummy was missing!

**Conversation pieces
from an eternal living room**

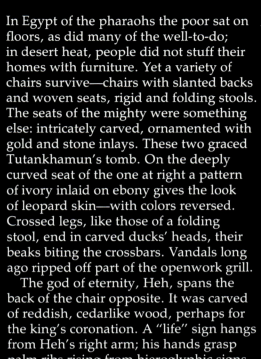

In Egypt of the pharaohs the poor sat on floors, as did many of the well-to-do; in desert heat, people did not stuff their homes with furniture. Yet a variety of chairs survive—chairs with slanted backs and woven seats, rigid and folding stools. The seats of the mighty were something else: intricately carved, ornamented with gold and stone inlays. These two graced Tutankhamun's tomb. On the deeply curved seat of the one at right a pattern of ivory inlaid on ebony gives the look of leopard skin—with colors reversed. Crossed legs, like those of a folding stool, end in carved ducks' heads, their beaks biting the crossbars. Vandals long ago ripped off part of the openwork grill.

The god of eternity, Heh, spans the back of the chair opposite. It was carved of reddish, cedarlike wood, perhaps for the king's coronation. A "life" sign hangs from Heh's right arm; his hands grasp palm ribs rising from hieroglyphic signs for "100,000 years" and "infinity."

Classical Rome and 19th-century Europe copied Egyptian styles, and Egyptian techniques serve us yet: dovetail, miter, and mortise-and-tenon joints. A coffin from about 2700 B.C. had thin wooden layers pegged together—perhaps the first plywood. Finely rounded furniture legs hint of a lathe, though none has turned up.

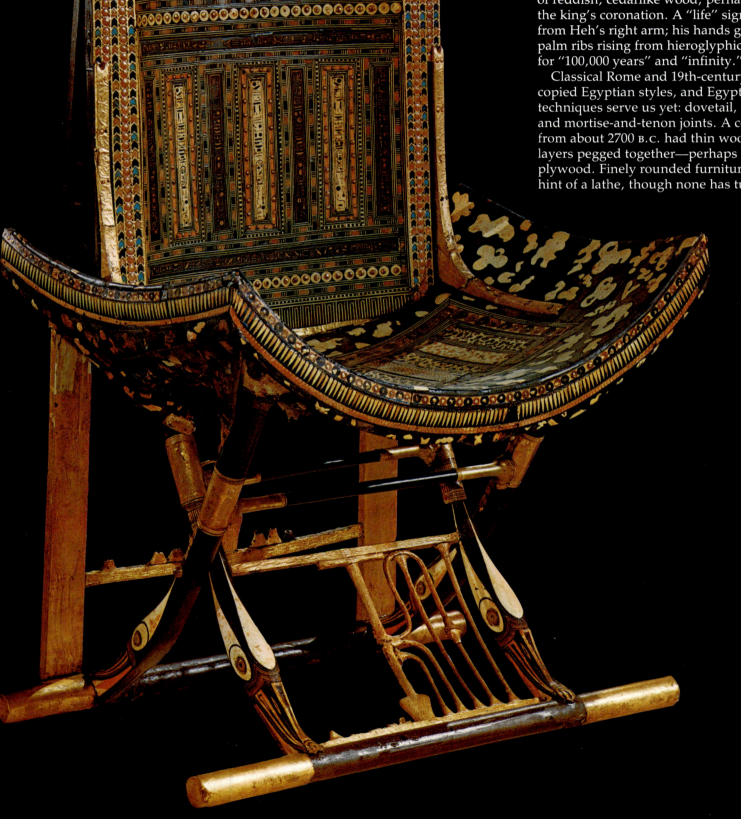

"That I may let you see my beauty in my . . . finest royal linen, when it is wet"

The poet in words, the sculptor in stone—each kindled New Kingdom senses with images still potent today. Sensuousness ripples across the lady in limestone; her pleated linen gown hugs every curve. She is thought to be the wife of Nakhtmin, an 18th-Dynasty nobleman.

Egyptians dressed lightly, mostly in white accented with rainbows of jewelry. A net of beads covers the white linen sheath of the offering bearer; her right hand pinions a live duck as the left steadies the drinking jars. She belongs to the charming troupe of wooden tomb models that livened the afterlife for the Middle Kingdom chancellor Meketre.

Children went naked; peasants wrapped a coarse cloth about their loins. A white kilt, modeled here by the Fifth-Dynasty overseer Methethy, symbolized status. Men wore kilts long or short, pleated or plain; one archeologist counted 40 styles. With a more complex society came more ornate clothing. By the New Kingdom the kilt had developed into a long skirt, and a nobleman's formal wear might include a shirt with wide pleated sleeves.

The masses walked barefoot, the rich in sandals. A king won a symbolic victory whenever he slipped them on. Royal sandals, such as these of Tutankhamun, had Egypt's enemies pictured on the inner soles.

The triumph of the *nuby* and the *neshdy*

Goldsmith and lapidary, creators of fine
jewelry, reached the peak of their art
in the Middle Kingdom. For Khnumet,
a princess of the 12th Dynasty, they wove
a diadem of delicate beauty—a scatter
of tiny flowers, strung on threads of gold,
gathered by crosses of papyrus blooms.
The wreath blends hues of semiprecious
stones: red carnelian, deep-blue lapis
lazuli, blue-green turquoise—the "classic
trio" of Egyptian lapidaries. Nile sailors
inspired the design. When stiff winds
tousled their hair, they wove weeds into
headbands. From the "boatman's circlet"
came Khnumet's dainty wreath—one of
the loveliest pieces ever found in Egypt.

To Khnumet, also, belonged this pendant.
On its medallion a cow rests against a
background of blue frit (a fuse of
ingredients similar to those of glass or
faience, cheaper than the imported lapis).
Its rosettes and stars are embellished
by granulation, a meticulous technique
which uses solder to fix tiny grains
of gold to a golden surface.

With the New Kingdom came new riches,
new styles. "In Egypt," wrote an Asian king,
"pure gold is the dust on the highroads."
Cascades of golden rosettes form this
headdress for a wife of Thutmose III.
She is not the model, and no one knows
just how it looked originally. Tomb
robbers of Qurna found it in pieces in
1916. The lady who wore it had $4\frac{1}{2}$ pounds
of gold and stones on her head. "Beauty,"
concluded archeologist Herbert Winlock,
"was taken seriously in ancient Egypt."

An ornament of enduring popularity

Ever in fashion, the broad collar appears
in every age, on men and women, living
and dead. Nefertari, beloved of Ramses II,
wears one in a painting; a serpent deity
squiggles through her pierced ear, and a
vulture goddess caps her head. For the
living a counterpoise tied at the back
prevented slipping; the dead had no need
of it. Hawks' heads form the shoulder
pieces of this collar strung with beads
of gold, carnelian, and feldspar.

Egyptian beads, unmatched in number
or variety by any other ancient culture,
exert a timeless lure. Long after the last
of the pharaohs, a guide for tomb robbers
bore the title *Book of Buried Beads and
Precious Treasures*. "Mummy beads," real
or fake, still dazzle the tourist's eye.

Jewels had magic: the charm of beauty
and the charm against evil. A mummy,
especially, needed protection. These three
rings, graven with gods, were among
15 found on the mummy of Tutankhamun.

The golden filling in a mud pie

Petrie found her tomb in 1914, her body broken, the amulets that guarded it gone. But off in a recess, roiled by floods and finally caked in mud, lay the jewels Sithathoryunet had worn as a princess of the 12th Dynasty. Little golden tubes, a thousand and more, sheathed the plaits of her wig. And on it sat this crown, golden plumes flashing and quivering with every step the princess took. The plumes are a token of the goddess Hathor, whose realm included love and beauty, the desert where gold and bright stones were found, and the miners who gathered them.

The crown's rosettes are worked in cloisonné—the technique of setting stone, faience, or glass within gold *cloisons*, or cells. Cloisonné jewelry, wrote the British scholar Cyril Aldred, "is the chief glory of Egyptian decorative art."

Feathers of cloisonné fill spread wings of the chest ornament from Tutankhamun's tomb. Above a fringe of flowers the pectoral centers on a falcon-winged scarab, composite symbol of the sun god. Falcon claws grasp "infinity" signs; scarab forelegs uphold the left Eye of Horus, symbol of the moon. On the silver moon disk, gilded deities flank the king.

The New Kingdom brought rigid bracelets into style. These, crafted for Ramses II, display two-headed birds and fine gold granulation. Hinges with movable pins made it easy to slip them on the wrists.

"Taking recreation,
seeing pleasant things. . ."

Nakht the hunter is a crack shot; his
throw sticks unerringly knock birds out
of the sky as he prepares another fling
at the flapping melee. His left hand holds
a decoy above the papyrus blind; a nude
son, wearing the sidelock of youth,
and an attendant pass the ammunition.
Nakht the fisherman, by contrast, is only
going through the motions. He has no

harpoon, though the fish wait patiently
in the bubble of water at his feet.

Nakht the scribe of the granaries in
the opulent 18th Dynasty surely had no
need to hunt to put meat on the table.
The hieroglyphs make clear the purpose of
this expedition: It is pure pleasure, a family
outing—the women lending a hand to

never completed, retains an amazing
freshness of color after 34 centuries.

The scene appears often in Egyptian art,
the lord of the tomb afloat on the
marshes, doubling as fowler and fisherman.
There is magic in it, a symbolic conquest
of hostile powers. But also, it expresses
the ageless yearning for a happy hunting

Senet, the national pastime

Everybody played senet. Menes, the traditional first pharaoh, knew the game. Nineteen dynasties and some 2,000 years later an artist showed Queen Nefertari sitting down to a game. A humble scribe who lived in her time was buried with the game board below, the playing pieces stored in the little drawer at the end. Tutankhamun must have loved the game; four sets went with him to the tomb. Temple workers scratched game grids on stone, schoolboys drew them on tablets.

The "blessed" ones could play on into eternity—so said the Book of the Dead. The senet board is also a hieroglyph, part of the word for "endure." Despite its enduring appeal, no one in modern times has discovered the rules of the game. The aim, apparently, was to move your flat or conical pieces through the 30 squares and off the board first. Moves depended upon the throw of "knucklebones" (on the board's left edge, below) or sticks. The scribe's board shows a 20-square game of Hyksos origin; the traditional version is on the bottom.

"Hounds and Jackals" vie on the ivory board in another popular game. Presumably the animal pieces raced from the trunk of the palm tree to the crown. By Coptic times an Egyptian die (bottom) had the array of spots we know today.

Any Egyptian could name that tune. It was their all-time hit: the Song of the Harper, a favorite, in varied form, through many centuries. People heeded its lyrics. There was music everywhere—in the air, wafting through the garden on the cooling north wind; in the morning at a rich lady's toilette; at dinner, and long after. Clappers kept rhythm while vintners stomped the grapes; pipers whistled a tune while farmers worked.

The harp, prized above all instruments, was patterned initially after the hunting bow. Often, as in this relief from the 18th Dynasty, a blind man played the harp. With time it added strings and grew in size until—in the reign of Ramses III—one model stood nearly seven feet high. Strings were tuned by winding them more or less tightly around the neck—the pegs used merely as fasteners.

Clappers, the earliest instruments recorded in Egypt, also evolved from a weapon. The earliest clappers had the bent shape of throw sticks. Hunters stalked the marshes, whacked their sticks together to flush the game, then fired them off for the kill. In time clappers

came to have the shape of hands. The three shown here were carved of wood and bone (lower). Tomb furnishings often included clappers to scare off evil spirits which, it was well known, had a phobia about noise. Clay rattles, such as those above, and the sistrum—often shaped like a cow's head and shaken in honor of Hathor or to soothe women in labor—added to the rhythm section.

Among the winds, the double clarinet (top), native to Egypt, has kept the same design for 4,700 years—from 2700 B.C. to the present day. The oboe next to it was of Asian origin. Oboes arrived in the New Kingdom, along with lyres, lutes, new harps—and skilled instrumentalists to play them. The New Kingdom orchestra must have been noisier, more exciting to listen to than the earlier ensembles. The melodies did not linger to our time. People played by ear, without notation. An Egyptian trumpet seems to be the only ancient instrument that sounds today as it did to the people who made it. The notes have been likened to a melancholy mooing. To Plutarch, 19 centuries ago, it sounded like the braying of an ass.

Heel over head for the goddess Hathor

Weighted pigtails swing down, arms and legs fly up—harem girls reach a delicate balance in an acrobatic dance, its beat set by clapping hands. The harem leader dances bottom row, center, according to the hieroglyphs. Time has leached some of the color in this relief from the tomb of an Old Kingdom vizier. In later times dances like this one highlighted rituals in the cult of Hathor. "The Pharaoh comes to dance," proclaimed the performers. "Sovereign Lady . . . look how he leaps!"

Pulsing rhythm, youthful bodies so supple and firm—ah, that such visions would never end! This was the driving hope of the ancient Egyptians, and they bet much of their lives and their treasure to fulfill it. Yet the hope remained only that, for who had ever returned from the "land of silence" to affirm the reality? Better to enjoy the pleasures of life now, sang the harper: *Spend the day merrily!*

139

The Gift of Writing

William Kelly Simpson

It is to writings that you must set
your mind. . . . I do not see an office
to be compared with [that of the
scribe]. . . . I shall make you love books
more than your mother, and I shall place
their excellence before you.

Thus the bureaucrat Dua-Khety admonished his son Pepy some 4,000 years ago as they sailed south to place the boy in a school for scribes. In so doing, he recognized a central fact of life in ancient Egypt: Though most Egyptians could not read or write, writing was an essential element in their society. Hieroglyphs—pictures of animals and the human body, plus myriad other signs—covered the walls of temples and tombs. And hieratic script, the cursive form comparable to our handwriting, pervaded daily affairs. It filled rolls of papyri in government and commerce and covered the stucco boards of students.

Writing already had a long history in Egypt by Dua-Khety's day, for hieroglyphs appeared in early dynastic times, around 3100 B.C. Scholars believe writing began with pictographs, in which, say, a picture of an ox meant an ox. Next came pictures that represented sounds and concepts. In English, a classic example of this rebus principle pictures a bee and a leaf to convey the idea of *belief*. Egyptians probably adopted the principle from Mesopotamia, where Sumerians had formalized a system of pictographs. There, pictographs evolved into cuneiform, cryptic wedge-shaped signs pressed into clay tablets. But in Egypt, formal hieroglyphs remained little changed for millenniums.

Meanwhile, cursive hieratic developed as the practical tool of communication—first as the script of accountants, with only slight modifications from the hieroglyphs. Then, as it found wider application on papyrus, hieratic assumed a more stylized form. Finally, around 700 B.C., it developed into a shorthand called demotic. Even when the Egyptians themselves eventually forgot how to read hieroglyphs, the demotic script never lost touch with its origins in the pictographs. Thus Egyptian writing preserved a language that, when rediscovered in the 19th century, revealed the history of a great civilization.

The writing also has a tie to us. Sinai workers, mining turquoise for Egyptian masters, put hieroglyphs to alphabetic use in their written language. Scholars tenuously trace some symbols from there into the Phoenician alphabet, ancestor of our own. So our writing, though not our language, has roots in the hieroglyphs.

The ancient Egyptians called their writing "words of the god," a gift of Thoth, the ibis-headed god of learning and writing. Later, the Greeks coined a word that preserved the meaning, hieroglyph—*hieros* (sacred), *glyphein* (to carve). To master the mysteries of the hieroglyphs was to be a scribe.

Scribal teachers poured scorn upon all other kinds of work. Students, usually the sons of officials who were expected to follow in their fathers' footsteps, were reminded that the tenant farmer saw the profit squeezed from his harvest by the landowner. The soldier had to go abroad and leave his family to the mercy of the tax collector. Dua-Khety, in the timeless manner of fathers counseling sons, hammered home the point. "The barber shaves until the end of evening. . . . The bricklayer . . . works outside in the wind with only a loincloth. . . . The weaver . . . is more wretched than a woman, his knees drawn up against his belly." But a scribe! He is, says one papyrus from around 1200 B.C., "the taskmaster of everyone."

Though many a boy might be trained at home by a tutor, the youth of means often went away to a scribal

Egypt's indispensable man

A scribe, still pinching a long-lost pen, sits in traditional cross-legged position, his tightly drawn kilt serving as a desk to hold a roll of papyrus. A masterpiece of Egyptian statuary found in a tomb at Saqqara in 1850, the limestone figure now in the Louvre dates from about 2500 B.C. It may represent Kai, a provincial governor during Dynasty 5 who, like many officials, sought to be remembered for his writing skills.

Spelling with pictures

Hieroglyphs usually combine ideograms (signs of things or ideas) with phonograms (signs that indicate sounds). A determinative—a sign to clarify meaning—is sometimes added. On this coffin lid from the fourth century B.C. (opposite), the name of a goddess can be found at the blue sign of the three-tiered throne in the far column. The throne is a phonogram, *st*. Adding vowels translates it into Aset, the Egyptian name for Isis. The half circle and the egg signify female. On the Dynasty 18 sarcophagus of King Amunhotep II (left), the throne resting on the kneeling woman's head readily identifies her as Isis. But in the column facing her, the same symbol preceded by an eye and followed by the seated "god" symbol changes the meaning to Osiris. The detail below, taken from the column behind her, spells out her prayer to the earth god Geb for the dead king: "Illumine his face, open his eyes."

Hook sign and long-handled mace, phonograms for *s* and *hd*, spell the word for illumine, *shd*. The sun is a determinative, the basket a masculine suffix for "you." Literally, "May you illumine."

Face ideogram has value of *hr* and also means *face*. Vertical rod signals "here symbol means what it depicts."

Horned viper is masculine suffix *-f* and signifies "he," "him," or "his."

Desert hare stands for the sound *wn*—the word for "open"—reinforced by the wavy water symbol *n*. Two determinatives follow: Door on its side indicates "open," forearm holding stick adds the idea of "force" or "effort."

Basket: masculine suffix for "you." Coupled with preceding group, it makes the five signs read, "May you open."

One eye is an ideogram that can stand for "see." But two indicate the "eyes" themselves. This pair have the phonetic value of *irty*.

Horned viper: "his." Diagonal strokes indicate the duality of "his eyes."

cultivated figs in it and grapes, and more wine than water. Its honey was abundant, and its olive trees numerous. . . . I spent many years while my offspring became strong men, each man managing his tribe."

But troubles interrupt Sinuhe's peaceful existence. He helps the prince against unfriendly tribes and at one point is challenged to single combat by an envious rival. The episode anticipates the Biblical story of David and Goliath: "There came a strong man of Retenu to challenge me in my tent. He was a champion without equal and had defeated all of Retenu. . . . He took up his shield, his ax, and his armful of javelins. . . . I made his arrows pass by me. . . . I shot him, my arrow fixed in his neck. He shouted and fell upon his nose."

Although successful in his new life, Sinuhe longs for home. He does not want to die abroad and be buried in a ram's skin instead of receiving the elaborate Egyptian burial rites and mummification. He decides to return to Egypt if the new king, Sesostris, will pardon his unauthorized flight.

The king welcomes Sinuhe back in a magnificent homecoming. "Years were caused to pass from my body. I was shaved, and my hair combed out. . . . I was outfitted with fine linen and rubbed with the finest oil. I passed the night on a real bed."

The king constructs a tomb for him with an inscribed and decorated chapel, and Sinuhe happily waits for the "day of mooring," his death. The story has many elements of interest: a description of Palestine around 1960 B.C., the resourcefulness of the Egyptian abroad, Sinuhe's touching homesickness and his reluctance to be interred far away with barbarous burial customs.

No group of literary works was more prized than the instructions of the great sages. In the maxims of the vizier Ptahhotep, the aging official begs the king to allow him to take his son as his assistant and successor. The king agrees but advises Ptahhotep to instruct his son properly: "Speak to him, for there is none born wise." Whereupon Ptahhotep writes: "If you find a disputant arguing, one having authority and superior to you,

Papyrus—creation of genius

Communication quickened in the ancient world with the invention of paper made from papyrus. Superior to the heavy, bulky, clay tablets of cuneiform writing, papyrus paper was thin, strong, flexible, easily carried, and conveniently stored. *Cyperus papyrus* (opposite), a marsh reed of the Nile, furnished the raw material.

First, workers harvested the stalks, as shown in the detail from the tomb of Nefer at Saqqara (above). Then papermakers peeled off the bark and cut the stems into foot-long pieces. Slicing thin strips lengthwise from the pith, they laid them—probably on a cloth—side by side and slightly overlapping (right). On these they superimposed more strips at right angles, covered them with another cloth, and with a mallet beat the assembled strips. The pounding interlocked cells of the strips, making a solid sheet. Then the sheet was set out to dry. A stone, shell, or piece of wood polished it smooth. To form rolls, sheets were stuck edge to edge with a flour paste.

On just what day some inspired Egyptian pounded out the first sheet of paper from papyrus is unknown, but scholars have found an unused roll in a Dynasty 1 tomb at Saqqara. Papyrus spread throughout the eastern Mediterranean, and for 4,000 years it fed the growth of civilizations. So vital was papyrus to the Romans that Tiberius rationed it during a shortage.

Conservation-minded Egyptians often scoured sheets clean for re-use. Their practice of recycling old paper into mummy casings proved a boon to classical scholars. In some casings they found early copies of Plato.

After cheaper pulp paper introduced from China became popular in the Middle Ages, Egyptians abandoned the making of papyrus and lost the art. But in 1962 Hassan Ragab, an Egyptian engineer and former diplomat, began experiments that led him back toward the original method. Today his Papyrus Institute in Cairo turns out papyrus similar to that of his ancestors. With only slightly modernized tools, institute workers hand-made the sample attached to this page from plants cultivated on an island in the Nile.

Ancient Egyptians found more than paper in *Cyperus papyrus*. In a land with relatively few trees, the all-purpose plant became a substitute for wood. People burned the root for fuel or carved it into utensils, and fashioned small boats from bundled reeds. They also plaited the inner bark into rope, and wove it into sailcloth, blankets, and baskets—perhaps one cradled the infant Moses. They even cooked and ate the plant.

Pliny the Elder reported that dried papyrus was used to heal boils, and that the ash from burned paper, "taken in wine, induced sleep."

Little wonder that Lower Egypt early made the plant its official emblem.

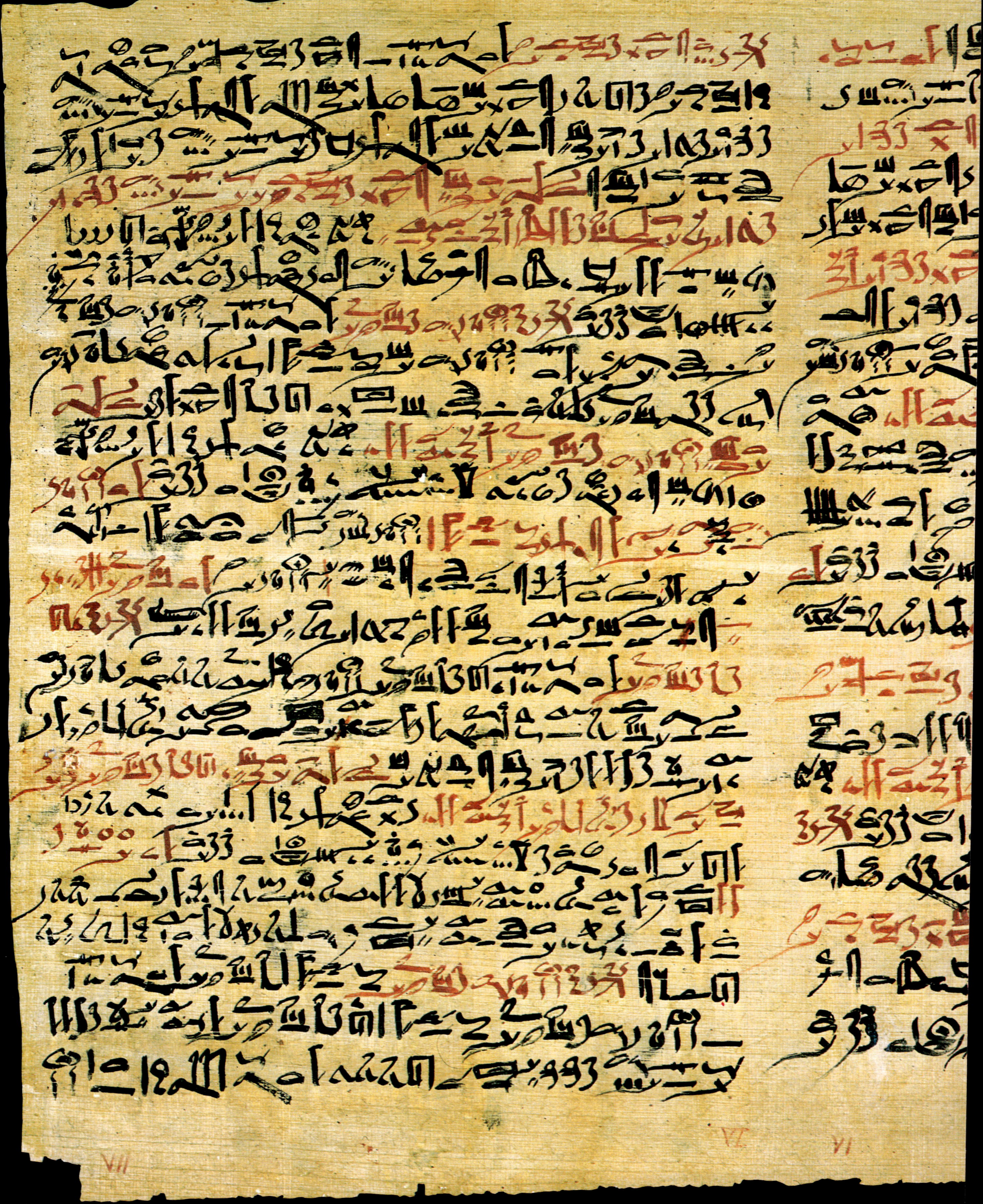

Hieratic: Speedwriting spreads the word

From earliest times scribes rounded off hieroglyphic symbols into a handwriting called hieratic. Using instruments similar to those below found in Tutankhamun's tomb—ivory palette with brushes and ink cakes, wooden brush holder, and ivory burnisher for smoothing papyrus—they employed the cursive script for commonplace documents. The folded letter (right) from Hekanakhte, a landowner of Dynasty 11, is addressed in hieratic to "The overseer of the Delta, Hrunufe." Hieratic also records early medical treatment in the Surgical Papyrus (opposite). Dating from 1700 B.C. but based on writings from the Old Kingdom, the cases were probably drawn up by an army surgeon: "One having a wound in his temple. An ailment which I will treat. . . .bind it with fresh meat the first day, and . . . treat afterward with grease and honey every day until he recovers."

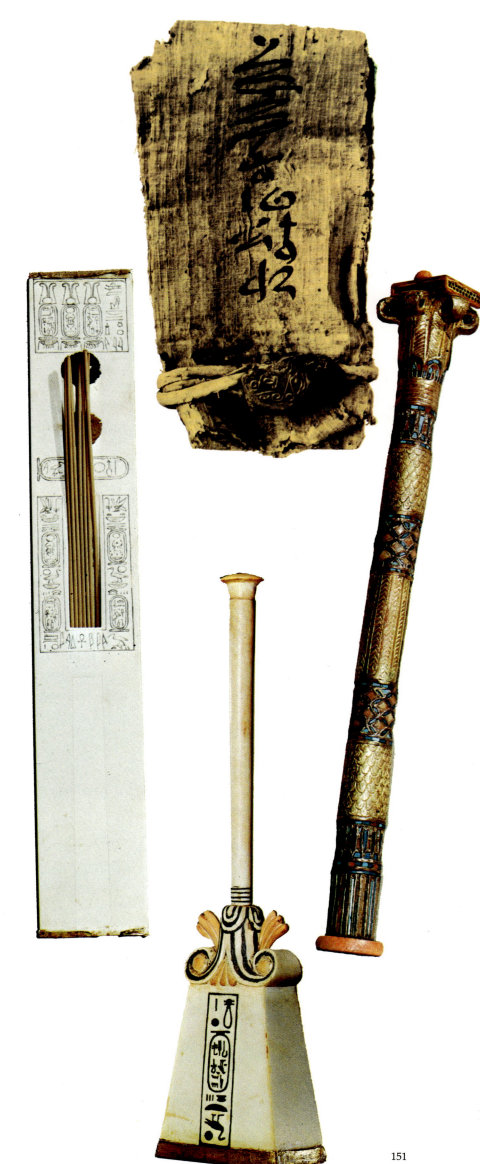

bend down your arms and bow your back; if you disagree with him, he will not side with you. . . .

"If you desire to preserve friendship in a home into which you enter, whether as lord or as brother or as friend . . . beware of approaching the women, for no good comes to a place where this is done. . . .

"If you desire your conduct to be good, refrain . . . from all kinds of evil. Beware of an act of avarice; it is a bad and incurable disease. . . . it alienates fathers and mothers . . . it drives wife and husband apart. . . .

"Do not repeat slander. . . . Repeat only a matter seen, not what is heard."

A thousand years later, the 30-chapter "Instruction of Amunemope" also emphasized proper conduct and ethical dealings. Some of the passages parallel those of the Old Testament's Book of Proverbs.

"Give your ears and hear what is said, give your mind over to their interpretation: It is profitable to put them in your heart." (Proverbs 22:17: "Bow down thine ear, and hear the words of the wise, and apply thine heart unto my knowledge.")

"Beware of stealing from a miserable man and of raging against the cripple." (Proverbs 22:22: "Rob not the poor . . . neither oppress the afflicted.")

Under the New Kingdom, Egypt entered upon an era of cosmopolitanism. Campaigns in Dynasties 18 and 19 penetrated the Levant to conquer or to maintain economic domination. Now, in literature, the soldier replaced the administrative official as a kind of cultural hero. In the tale of "The Doomed Prince," the theme, like that of Sinuhe, deals with the Egyptian abroad.

At the prince's birth several goddesses predict that he will be killed by a crocodile, a snake, or a dog. His father, the king, keeps him safe from these dangers in his youth. But when the prince grows up, he becomes restless for adventure and sets off in his warrior's chariot for the Land of the Two Rivers. At the court of the Prince of Naharain, he wins the hand of the nobleman's daughter by outdoing the sons of other princes in a leaping contest.

Pyramid Texts—open sesame to eternity
Wall-to-wall words of magic fill the antechamber of the Pyramid of Unas at Saqqara. Oldest example of the Pyramid Texts, these "Utterances" helped launch Unas, last king of Dynasty 5, on his perilous journey through the underworld to his place among the gods. Pyramid Texts—funerary literature inscribed in pyramid burial chambers of Dynasties 5 and 6—preserve Egypt's earliest known religious beliefs. Utterances describe the hereafter, offer rituals for the dead, and repeat spells, or incantations, against evil. Hieroglyphic symbols are sometimes altered to neutralize possible peril: the scorpion without its tail and humans lacking bodies and legs.

As a formal script, hieroglyphs changed little through the ages. A thousand years after the Pyramid Texts, Unas would have understood the characters on the Dynasty 18 steatite scarab of Amunhotep III (left). Medallions commemorating the king's latest project, scarabs were circulated like newsletters. This one, measuring more than three inches long, tells of an irrigation project created in honor of Amunhotep's queen, Tiy.

One evening as the young Egyptian sleeps, a snake appears. His wife has set out bowls of wine and beer; the snake drinks and gets drunk, and the wife chops it to pieces with an ax. Later, the youth's greyhound tries to bite him. He flees to the lake, only to encounter a crocodile, who tells him his life will be spared if he can overcome the crocodile's enemy, a water spirit.

Here the manuscript breaks off. Let's assume a happy ending for the "doomed" prince. Egyptians firmly believed that good could triumph over evil.

Mythology abounds in the tale of "The Two Brothers." Humans change into animals and animals talk. And again we find an incident that parallels a Biblical episode, the story of Joseph and Potiphar's wife.

Anubis and his wife live on a farm with his brother Bata. One day when Bata returns from the fields to fetch seed, his sister-in-law suggests they make love while her husband is still out working. Bata refuses and rejoins his older brother. When Anubis returns to the house, his wife tells him Bata tried to rape her. Angered, Anubis hides in the stable to kill Bata.

At sunset Bata returns with the cattle. "The lead cow entered the stable and said . . .: Look, your elder brother is standing in wait for you, bearing his spear to kill you." Bata flees. Eventually, Anubis learns the truth, kills his wife, and casts her body to the dogs.

From this point on, the storyteller's account takes one bizarre turn after another. Bata goes off to Lebanon and places his own heart in the top of a pine tree, having arranged with Anubis to put it in a bowl of cool water if evil befalls him.

In Lebanon, the gods fashion a beautiful wife for Bata. Soon the sea carries a lock of her hair to Egypt. Its scent becomes mixed with the pharaoh's laundry, and he sends out expeditions to find the owner of the hair. In due course, the wife deserts Bata for the pharaoh, who has the pine tree cut down. Bata dies.

Prompted by strange events at home, Anubis seeks out his brother's heart and restores Bata to life. Bata changes himself into a bull in order to kill his wife. She slays the bull, but Bata lives on in two trees that spring up from his blood. When she learns of Bata's new identity, she cuts down the trees, accidentally swallows a flying splinter, and becomes pregnant. Bata is reborn as her son, the crown prince. When the pharaoh dies, Bata ascends the throne, judges his mother/wife, and appoints Anubis his successor.

This story may have been invented to reflect an intrigue at court or to elaborate on the lives of the gods, for Anubis and Bata were familiar deities. Rich and vivid, it is also complicated, in sharp contrast to the simple directness of Egyptian love poetry, seen in these examples from New Kingdom times.

Seven days . . . and I've not seen my lady love.
A sickness has shot through me.
I have become sluggish,
And I have forgotten my own body.
If the best surgeons come to me,
My heart will not be comforted with their remedies. . . .
My lady love is more remedial than any potion;
She's better than the whole book of medical lore. . . .
If I see her, then I'll be well. . . .

Distracting is the foliage of my pasture:
The mouth of my girl is a lotus bud,
Her breasts are mandrake apples,
Her arms are vines,
Her eyes are fixed like berries,
Her brow a snare of willow, and I the wild goose!

This poetry from ancient Egypt, like the wondrous tales and the serious instructions, deserves to be better known. We are familiar with the pyramids, the great temples, the marvelous bust of Queen Nefertiti, the treasures of Tutankhamun. But few people know the enchantment of the stories or the insight into distant times provided by such literary works. The world of Egypt belonged to the kings and the gods with their tombs and temples. But it also belonged to the scribe and the written word, the hieroglyphs.

Pathways to the Gods

Virginia Lee Davis

Take to yourself the Eye of Horus
That you may gain power through it,
That you may gain peace through it
And become a living being, foremost of the gods.

That was the Egyptian formula for immortality. We may not recognize the reference to the eye of a god. But we can see here an idea: transformation. And we can see in "gain power" and "gain peace" the steps leading toward transformation. That inscription could also proclaim the Egyptians' faith in the durability of their monuments. They tried to make their temples and tombs into time capsules for eternity.

The buildings were meant to survive forever and maintain the proper conditions that would ensure fulfillment of the Egyptians' deepest belief. It was a belief we can translate into a bold declaration: "You have not gone away dead. You have gone away alive!"

We see the temple as a house of worship for a god and the tomb as a burial place for a mortal. To us, each building has a different sort of owner as well as a different purpose. Egyptians did not think that way. To them, the gods and human beings did not differ very much. Both had need of a tomb as well as a temple.

This is fortunate for the modern investigator of Egyptian religion. The temples and tombs of men are the more numerous and also the better preserved. Insights discovered in them can be applied to the few and usually battered temples and tombs of the gods.

To an ancient Egyptian, every temple was a miniature replica of Egypt itself and every tomb was a replica of the primeval mound of creation. Everywhere the people could see and feel their religion. And the gods were real, as real as mortal beings.

Enough stones still stand so that we can envision, in the ruins of temples and tombs, what was built by the religion of the Egyptians. But time has worn away the spiritual bridges between them and us. Our eyes are not their eyes, and our minds are not their minds. Yet, to understand the Egyptians, we must learn about the religion that was the center of their lives. We must try to span the gulf between their time and our time, between their thought and our thought.

When we compare our religions to Egyptian religion, we usually don't compare the right things. We want to compare our belief in God to their gods, our kings to their kings. We should compare our God to their kings and their gods to angels and demons.

They saw their gods every hour of the day and night, in sun and moon and stars, in the Nile and its cliffs, in flowers and in animals. And in human beings, for the goal of their religion was the transformation of human beings into gods—or gods into human beings.

Their religion was administered by a bureaucracy under the pharaoh. Officials of the central and local governments could have both political and religious duties. A director of public works might also be a chief of priests. The priests he directed would also be double jobholders. They might work tilling in the fields—and, when called upon, perform work in the temple.

The few ordinary people involved in services were servants, not worshipers. Most Egyptians participated in religion by labor or through "endowments," a kind of tithing with grain, cattle, or other valuables.

It was a living religion. And behind its complex theology lay basic beliefs not drastically different from some of ours. Most of us believe in a relationship between God and human beings. We read in the Bible that we were made in God's image and that we are the "sons of the living God." Noting similarities between Egyptian thought and ours does not detract from the Bible's teachings. We are merely making observations. What we personally believe is another matter.

We observe, for example, that, like us, Egyptians wondered how to deal with the environment. To them, mother nature was unruly and human civilization was orderly. The Egyptians saw this reality in terms of conflict. Heedless nature had to be controlled if people were to build, in the realm of nature, a realm of man: a social order, cities, a nation.

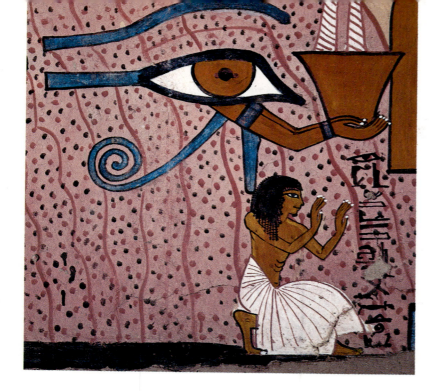

"Hail to you, O Eye of Horus"

The Sacred Eye, "which leads on the road of darkness," hovers over a dead man in his tomb. He will be ushered into the underworld by the eye, whose mystical hands hold a bowl of flaming incense. Torn from the great god Horus by his foe Seth, the eye was recovered by Horus's friend, the god Thoth, and became a symbol for things lost and found again, for things made more precious by having been restored. Symbols filled tombs, temples—and minds—of Egyptians. The hieroglyphic sign for Horus was the falcon, bird of all-seeing eyes. As a bird symbol, Horus soared back in time, for the oldest sky deities were falcons.

The Egyptians' religion gave them a way to reconcile nature and civilization. The gods had to be tamed and taught to look after the interests of human beings. And people had to learn to be wily enough to take care of themselves and cope with nature.

Temples and tombs were terminals in this ceaseless shuttling between divine and human. No being was complete until it had passed through both transformations as god and man. The transformation of man into god took place within the tomb; the transformation of god into man took place within the temple.

The tombs were the province of gods, who would free the dead from human limitations. The temples were places where people would school the gods in human ways. This idea of vice versa, of things working conversely, ran through Egyptian thought. In fact, one of their frequently used expressions can be translated as "vice versa."

Religion was a rhythm of faith. It resounded in the rituals of tomb and temple. It was a faith that could be seen in symbols and in realities, a faith that tried to achieve a balancing of the powers of heaven and earth. Religion became a veritable way of life, its influence extending to every aspect of human endeavor.

We cannot now "explain" that religion any more than we can fully explain the Christianity of the Middle Ages. Can we fully explain how the Cross symbolizes the entire Christian ethic? We try. And perhaps by trying to understand the Egyptian concept of a single important symbol—the Sacred Eye—we can understand a basic concept of Egyptian religion: the quest for the ideal person.

The ideal person was a composite of parts, and so was the Sacred Eye. Indeed, the eye's name, *udjat*, meant complete, in the sense of having all parts present and accounted for. People wore Sacred Eye amulets to help ensure that they would be complete, with all parts attached and all faculties in good condition. There is an echo of Egyptian thought about "parts" of a person in some of our slang expressions: "He doesn't

have all his buttons," "He's got a screw loose," and "She's just not all there."

The Sacred Eye, the most common and still the most mysterious of countless Egyptian symbols, owed its shape to visualizations of the powerful sky god Horus, who had the sun and moon for eyes. He was also what we call the Milky Way and was portrayed as an elongated human, a star-spotted cheetah, or a giant falcon with outstretched wings. So the eyes of Horus could combine the characteristic markings of all three species: the long eyebrow of a human being, the coiled "tear-stripes" on the face of a cheetah, and the tiny cheek-marks of a falcon.

According to a myth about the phases of the moon, the wicked god Seth plucked out the eye of Horus and tore it to bits. But the wise god Thoth stuck it back together again—as if it were just a cracked grain of barley. And so each part of the eye became a hieroglyphic sign for a fraction used in measuring out bushels of grain: ◁ for $1/2$; ○ for $1/4$; ⌒ for $1/8$; ⌓ for $1/16$; ↘ for $1/32$; ◖ for $1/64$. When the fraction symbols are put together, the marvelously restored "sound eye" looks like the symbol shown in this paragraph. (Note that if you add up the fractions, your answer is only $63/64$. The missing $1/64$ was the bit of magic needed for cement, the miraculous stuff that makes a dead eye shine again with life!)

In the Sacred Eye, the Egyptians saw the six parts of a well-rounded personality, plump with every sort of power, both heavenly and earthly. This was a creature able to control heaven and earth. Neither the gods in heaven nor people on earth could aspire to such greatness, for the gods lacked earthly bodies and men lacked heavenly powers. Only one person could achieve such perfection: the pharaoh. Other people and the gods, however, could do their part by furthering his interests, for the benefit of all. So it was the pharaoh who shone out of the Sacred Eye.

Since the Sacred Eye with its six parts symbolized a complete person, it seems to follow that a complete

Egyptian should also be analyzed as a six-fold thing. We know that the human body—as well as the human personality—can be divided into as many parts as a physician or a psychoanalyst cares to name. The Egyptians likewise came up with a good many names for "parts." But six words for parts of a person stand out in texts by virtue of their frequency and importance: ⎁ *ka*, 𓂝 *ba*, 𓄿 𓏏 *khat*, 𓏛 *ren*, 𓈖 *shut*, 𓅜 *akh*.

In what follows, I will be exploring the meaning and significance of these words, though I wish to stress that full understanding of them still eludes us.

There is, however, a beautifully simple approach. How do we recognize a person, an animal, or anything else? By sight, touch, hearing, taste, smell—or by plain old intuition. I suspect that, in Egyptian terms, each part of a being is whatever can be perceived by our five senses and that extra we call our sixth sense.

I suggest simply this: An Egyptian, contemplating a being, perceived its glowing color as its *akh*, its cool shadow as its *shut*, its name as its *ren*, the flavor of its flesh as its *khat*, its odor as its *ba*, and its inner and hidden nature as its *ka*.

Can the Sacred Eye stand for those six parts? I think it can. Using all six (!) senses in my study of Egyptian texts, I reach the following conclusions.

Let us start with the inner corner of the white of the eye, written as ◁. I think this symbolized the ka, the mold that begins the creative process. As this part of the eye cups and shapes the eye, so does the ka hold and guide the personality. For a pharaoh, his ka meant "My majesty has breeding." His lineage, then, by the value assigned to this symbol, was worth at least half of his personality. The first of Tutankhamun's five kingly names, for example, was "Strong bull, perfect of births." The many-worded name stressed the importance of the pharaoh's genetic heritage.

The pupil of the eye, ⬤, had a symbolic worth of one-quarter, an indication of how important to Egyptians was the quality they called the ba. The pupil does for the eye what the viscera does for the body: contains liquid. The ba, representing the inner power that determines the thrust of the personality, also said, in a way, "The pharaoh has guts."

The eyebrow, ⌒, with its one-eighth value, shelters the eye and bends to its every movement. So does the khat, the material substance that sustains the body. Flesh is a kind of khat, for it covers the bones, yet is always flexible. The khat shelters the pharaoh's personality. With their love of puns, the Egyptians would say of the khat, "The pharaoh is a weighty personage."

The outer corner of the eyewhite, ▷, moves with facial expressions, just as the lips move to the sound of a name. And so this eye part, with its one-sixteenth value, represents the ren, the name that characterizes the individual. Always it was said of the pharaoh, "He boasts a great name."

He also "casts a long shadow," and this is acknowledged in the fifth part of the personality, the shut—the dependent shadow that repeats its owner's proportions. The eye part that symbolizes this is the cheetah's tear-stripe, ⤵, for, just as the tear-stripe traces the track of tears expelled from the eye, so does the shadow follow the profile of shade cast by its owner.

The vital spirit that animates the personality is the akh, symbolized by the falcon's cheek-mark, ⧣. As the sharpness of the cheek-mark heightens the sharpness of the eye, so does the vitality of the spirit heighten the vitality of the owner. This sixth and final facet of the personality has the seemingly smallest value. But in this mere spark is the essence of life.

In these symbols-within-symbols—in the akh as well as in the ka, the ba, and other attributes of personality—Egyptians perceived still other symbols and imagery. Like modern psychiatrists with their probing of id (akh), ego (ren), and superego (ka), Egyptians searched for hidden meanings through wordplay and free association: Why is this word feminine and that word masculine? What does the moon make you think

In the dark of the tomb, life and light

The *ka*—what we might call our conscience or other self—seems to step through the wall of a House of Eternity. Egyptians believed that after death parts of the personality lingered in the tomb. At the feet of the ka were placed offerings on behalf of the body. Three parts of the deceased—the ka, the name, and the mummy—stayed close by. Other parts, such as the winged, soul-like *ba* and the black *shut*, wandered. We see them portrayed in tombs (right). The human-headed ba, a creature of night, flits across the sky with the stars. The inky black shut, shadow of the personality, stalks the dark halls of the mortuary temple. The shiny *akh*, spirit of light, follows the sun by day and returns at night to illumine the tomb with rays of hope.

of? What does the *word* for moon make you think of?

Take the ideas included in the akh, for example. The root-word has so many possible meanings that some authorities wonder if "akh" can even be translated. It may mean the act of being good, or effective, or agreeable, or sacred—or transfigured. The akh is even sometimes thought of as an adolescent girl! This is because akh and other words defining the personality have a connotation of kinship. The ka is "fatherly" and the akh is "daughter-like." From the akh, then, arose the image of an adolescent daughter. She is vital, passionate, sparkling with life—and subconsciously in love with her father.

Also locked within the akh is the idea of a controlling spirit. The idea can be seen by imagining a daughter being taken away from her father, for the good of both.

If you see this aspect of the akh as the stuff of myth and drama, you are beginning to think like an ancient Egyptian. The role-playing words that describe the personality do, in a mystical shorthand, act out religious myths. And from myth, from the magic of words—from the concept of the akh itself—comes the inspiration for Egyptian drama. It is a drama that swirls through the complex life-and-death world of Egyptian thought and religion. It is a drama we can recognize.

The Egyptians believed that a proper play should reflect universal truths. And, as sound dramatists, they realized that a play should be based upon events which ordinary people could understand. Dramatic enactments were basic to all Egyptian ritual. The enactments were associated with cosmic events. And to bring the cosmos down to earth, the Egyptians often used a theme everybody would recognize: robbery.

In the myth-filled drama of the heavens, robbery is what makes the universe go round. Just as a pharaoh loses his crown to a usurper, so does Venus lose its position near Sirius to the waxing moon. But the moon will be pushed aside by the immense sky. The Milky Way will dominate the sky. Then will come the sun, but it will be robbed by the clouds of twilight.

On earth, the drama is also give-and-take. The river in flood robs the banks, the towns and canals rob the muddy floodwater, the land robs mud from the water.

In the heavens and on the earth, events coincide. If everyone on earth performs his or her proper role in life, then everyone in heaven will—to use a favorite Egyptian expression—do likewise. Or, to use another one—and vice versa.

Temples and tombs, the theaters for ritual dramas, are the creations of an intellectual process rooted deep in the Egyptian consciousness. Before men built these stages of stone there was ritual itself—drama that inspired key details of temple and tomb. Before the ritual came the symbols that clothed even the sorriest actor with divine charisma. Before the symbols came the names that defined the character of every actor. Before the names came the images of the gods that filled the weakest actor with godly power. And before there were words or images, there was the source of it all: the primitive thoughts, the basic plots that assigned the roles to gods and people.

Inspiring the religion's complex, long-evolving drama was a simple desire: to solve all the problems and obtain all the comforts of life in this world and in the next. The favorable conditions of life in Egypt practically guaranteed satisfaction of at least part of this desire. And as long as such satisfaction repeated itself year after year, the Egyptians did not waver from belief in their religion. We can still see this faith in the complacent smiles on faces looking upon eternity: "You may rise like the sun, rejuvenate yourself like the moon, repeat life like the flood of the Nile."

The religion's ritual dramas varied little from time to time and place to place. Like the mystery plays of the Middle Ages, the Egyptian rituals were designed to instruct, not entertain. But, unlike performances of mystery plays, Egyptian ritual had no popular audience.

Its audience consisted of the gods themselves. The temple proper was off limits to ordinary people, unless they had been purified by the priests for the performance of specific temple duties.

The priestly actors, with the pharaoh at their head, impersonated such cosmic beings as the planets. But the events of the plays—as we can see in a papyrus "script" that survives—are simple human acts: from plowing and planting and reaping through hunting and fishing and warfare—and birth and death and embalming. The enactments anticipated the real events; the idea behind the play was to help shape these events for the benefit of all, both people and gods.

In what has become known as the Mystery Play of the Succession, the pharaoh enacts, in city after city, his assumption of office. It is a kind of coronation. But it is more than that. The pharaoh had to act out the drama in order for the real event to occur. In a description of a typical scene, the papyrus script sets forth the action in two ways—as a happening and as meaning:

> It happened that barley was put on the threshing floor.
> It happened that male animals were brought to trample it.
> [Stage direction: The animals—sheep and donkeys —are beaten by the officiating priest.]
> That means Horus avenging his father.

In Egyptian mythology, Horus, son of Osiris, battles Seth, the murderer of Osiris. Horus and Seth are rivals for the throne of Osiris. Though dead, Osiris is ruler of the world beyond and is resurrected as the seed that becomes grain, the river that floods, the moon that waxes and wanes. Horus avenges his father through an agricultural version of death and resurrection.

In the play, the pharaoh, portraying Horus, tells the animals not to trample the grain (a symbol of Osiris). The animals disobey. (The grain, after all, has to be threshed—sacrificed—if there is going to be any food.) Horus then symbolically beats the animals and, says the script, "Horus speaks to Osiris: 'I have beaten for you those who have beaten you.'"

Near the end of the play, the pharaoh passes out food. A stage direction in the script says: "A loaf of bread; a jug of beer." Thus does food and drink—both the products of "sacrificed" grain—come from the king-god to the people. Kings must die; grain must die. But sons come forth, as do beer and bread, the offspring of a successful harvest.

Only the initiated—officials, priests, royalty—were permitted near the pharaoh during a ritual. But the entire community participated in the feast and celebration as god—and king—paraded through town and country, renewing the intimate connection between heaven and earth and reaffirming the mutual dependence of the two realms.

Rituals everywhere became more and more similar as the priestly organizers improved their techniques and approached what they hoped would be the perfect ceremony. Not so the myths, however. The myths, in which the proper cosmic order is proclaimed, varied greatly from place to place and through the years.

Every important town had its own creator god and its own explanation of how he had made the universe. The environment had much to do with the explanation, and changes in the environment brought changes in the mythology. A gradual change in climate, a shift in political power—these were the typical forces that helped to reshape mythology.

In the marshy Delta area of Lower Egypt, where the perennial task was dealing with wetlands, the people generally turned for aid to the solar gods: the sun, the planets, and the dusty wind off the desert. In the arid valley area of Upper Egypt, where the problem was

A royal barge voyages through time

This 140-foot vessel, buried 4,500 years ago and discovered in 1954, is the oldest ship ever found. Such a ship probably bore the body of Pharaoh Cheops from his capital at Memphis to Giza, site of his Great Pyramid. Stowed nearby for afterlife cruising, it was taken apart and some of its 1,220 pieces were marked with shipwrights' directions for reassembly. In restoration, the ship was virtually sewed together with thousands of feet of rope, per direction. Its timber came from the Biblical cedars of Lebanon.

dealing with dry lands, aid was sought from the lunar gods: the moon, the sky itself, and the Milky Way.

Politically, the historical pattern was for southerners to unite Upper and Lower Egypt—the Two Lands— and then to move north, reigning in a capital in the vicinity of Memphis. There the southerners would come under the influence of northern culture and would respond to peculiarly northern problems until they themselves turned into northerners. Or were replaced by a new wave of rulers from the south.

A theological shift accompanied the political one. The changeover from lunar to solar worship first developed in the Third Dynasty. The solar theology culminated in the Fifth Dynasty when it became a matter of doctrine that all pharaohs were "sons of the sun." (Because of their love of—and reverence for—puns, Egyptians would enjoy the coincidence in the sound and appearance of those English words.)

Famine and disorder in the First Intermediate Period put solar worship into eclipse. The sun's prestige was never quite the same. Not until the beginning of the Second Intermediate Period did solar worship revive in the Delta. The revival coincided with the coming of Asiatics and a breakdown in authority at Memphis.

The founding of the 18th Dynasty and the beginning of the New Kingdom brought a resurgence of lunar worship. At the same time, the Valley of the Kings became a royal burial place and temples began rising at Thebes. Not until the end of this dynasty did solar worship once more gain precedence.

During later dynasties, Egypt prospered under the protection of Re, the sun god, and Shu, god of the air and bearer of the heavens. And it is from this era that we get a rare and explicit statement about proper order in the universe:

" 'As for Egypt,' 'tis said since the time of the gods,

"Imperishable Stars" sail the northern sky

Divine constellations cruise the lively night, painted on the ceiling of a burial chamber. Hippopotamus and crocodile precede the goddess Isis. Egyptians split the sky into southern and northern parts, with the Milky Way as the dividing line. They called some stars "untiring" because they ceaselessly rose and set on the horizon. Some were seen as sailors of The Ship, probably our Pegasus. Stars wheeling around the northern sky never set and were "imperishable." These (right) included the bull Meskhetiu, which corresponds to our Big Dipper. Some stars that form our Little Dipper appear in the falcon-headed human who, below the bull, tugs on the axis of the world.

'she's Re's only daughter, and he on the throne of Shu is his son, and no wits suffice to defeat her people, for every god's eye is after her spoilers; herself she'll defeat all her enemies,' say they who look to their stars and know all their spells from gazing on winds."

Egyptians looked to the skies for much of their symbolism. The moon was a white skull, the sun a red face. They saw the night sky as a milk-filled udder. But what we call the Milky Way they saw as an elongated torso. As writing developed, its hieroglyphic signs became sacred and often poetic symbols-for-symbols. The sign for the sun looked like one of their numerous pills. In the winding sign for Milky Way an Egyptian would perceive a writhing serpent. The moon sign resembled a scimitar to slit open the serpent's belly.

To symbolize a cosmic being with tiny hieroglyphic signs was to reduce his awesome powers to manageable earthly dimensions. And to symbolize an earthly being as a composite of all the cosmic entities was to magnify his feeble powers into cosmic dimensions. If the signs were well chosen and evocatively designed, the powers of the heavens would be captured in caricatures made by human beings. Belief in the potency of symbols was a basic tenet of Egyptian religion.

Though the symbols themselves did not often change, the things they represented did. The original eye symbol, for example, was called Iris ("the active eye") and represented the star Sirius. At first Iris was an eye at the edge of the lunar profile. When the moon's path took it near the star, the moon was said to have regained its lost eye. This produced the brilliance of the harvest moon in October.

With the shift to solar worship, all the same symbolism was transferred to the sun. Now it was the *sun* that took a path near the star, regained its lost eye—and attained the blazing power of the summer sun of June.

Eventually, as a pair of eyes came to represent these cosmic events, the symbolism underwent change. The left eye's inner eyewhite looked like the first crescent of the moon as seen in the west at sunset, heralding the beginning of night. The right eye's inner eyewhite looked like the last crescent of the moon in the east at sunrise, promising day.

The left eye, called *mehit* ("the full eye"), became the symbol of the moon; the right eye, *udjat* ("the whole eye"), represented the sun. They were then attributed to the sky god, Horus of the Two Horizons, "amidst the sky, with day his right eye and night his left."

Egyptian imagery was inspired by a belief that paralleled the faith in symbols: Something imagined could produce something real. A proper image reflected a being's power. And the best images, like the best symbols, were to be found in the heavens.

Our eyes see Egyptian images as beautiful and unfathomable. We look at things literally. Yet, hidden in our minds are perceptions beyond sight. We need only a prod from a psychologist to see fantasies in an ink blot. The Egyptian, with the double vision of religion, saw both the object portrayed and, beyond the portrayal, not fantasy but reality.

Look with Egyptian eyes—and see! A pair of swimming cows, only their curving horns visible? See the curves of both horizons circling the vast expanse of a watery blue sky. A pair of cobras, one rearing and one striking? See in their beady eyes and eye-like markings on their hoods the blazing disks of the rising and the setting sun. Now look with insight upon a sacred ibis of snowy plumage, poised to snatch a fish—and see reflected the pale sheen of the moon as it swallows the stars in its path across the sky. A great crocodile with hooded eyes glides through the swamps, evoking the Milky Way's shining grace as it sweeps through the night. Sharp-eyed falcons climbing or stooping in flight re-enact the motions of the planets in their strange wanderings.

Showing earthly beings with cosmic shapes injected the ordinary with mysterious powers. And giving cosmic beings earthly shapes infected the powerful with the weaknesses of their earthly counterparts.

One of the most powerful images is that of the fal-

Overleaf: And in southern skies, stars are born

The heavenly body of the sky goddess spans the ceiling of the tomb of Ramses VI, encompassing the Book of Day (lower) and the Book of Night, god-filled chronicles of the cosmos. Her body represents the sun's path, artistically equated with the Milky Way, though Egyptian astronomers knew better. Into her mouth in the west each night goes the sun, which passes through her body—note the red disks—and is born from her at dawn. She also swallows the stars—they look like asterisks—and gives birth to them at night. Egyptians invented the 24-hour day but, loving symmetry, split it in half. Thus each of the 12 daylight hours was longer in summer than in winter—and, for night, vice versa.

con. The pharaoh is Horus, and his image is the falcon, which combines within itself the dark colors of the sky, the downy shadows of the earth, the soaring motions of the Milky Way, the swooping orbits of the planets, and a pair of shining eyes for the sun and moon.

Of all the changes that occurred in Egyptian imagery, the greatest was from purely animal forms, through half-human forms, to purely human forms. Such changes went along with the evolution of an urban culture and an increase in population. People competed with animals for space until finally man's only competitor was man and the animal world ceased to be of much importance.

Improvements in tools and technology also had their effect on the details and quality of the images. But no matter the era or the place, manufactured images always were accompanied by living images. These might be certain animals, such as bulls revered in their temple stables as living manifestations of the gods. Similarly, a pharaoh was revered in his palace, built near the site of his proposed mortuary temple.

Both divine animal and divine king were mummified at death and carefully stored away for all eternity. After earthly death, such creatures were believed capable of assuming any form at will.

In "spells"—texts found on coffins—we can read of such changes:

> *Being transformed into a divine falcon. . . .*
> *Taking shape as a falcon. . . .*
> *Becoming a human falcon. . . .*
> *Assuming all forms in the realm of the dead. . . .*
> *Taking shape as Hathor* [a sky goddess often
> portrayed as a cow] *in the realm of the dead. . . .*
> *Becoming Sobek* [a crocodile god], *lord of the
> Winding Waterway. . . .*
> *Taking shape as any god that a man may wish. . . .*

To Egyptians, much was possible because they believed in something that would sound familiar to us: "The word is father to the thought." And if one par-

ticular word was right, it would foster a rightness with the universe. That particular word was the name, the ren, of an individual. The feeling was summed up in an inscription: "I am hale and also my flesh; it goes well with me and with my name."

A name had to reflect the character of its owner, and the owner was expected to live up to the name. As usual, the place to look for the best names was in the sky, among the rightly named cosmic beings.

The wider-ranging a name, the greater the effect on a being's character, and the more double meanings or puns, the more power. A resounding example can be found in the name of the great god Amun. Now there was a name that echoed in the heavens!

Representing the hieroglyphic signs for "Amun" as the letters *i m e n* in our alphabet, we can take the god's name apart and look inside it, Egyptian-style. This means looking for anagrams. We find creator (*imen*), herder (*mien*), shelterer (*inem*), shouter (*nemi*), grasper (*meni*), and wanderer (*niem*).

At first nearly every province in Egypt had its own name for its creator god. As the country was unified, each successive unifier brought into prominence his own local creator god. The sun god Re of Heliopolis—"City of the Sun"—attained his greatest power during the Old Kingdom. His power radiates in the names of pharaohs: Khafre (Chephren) is made of signs that mean "Re is his glory," and Menkaure (Mycerinus) translates as "Enduring is the solicitude of Re." Two of the wondrous pyramids at Giza rose as monuments to the greatness of those pharaohs.

But Re faltered. The Old Kingdom fell, and the records lamented: "The wrongdoer is everywhere. . . . The robber is a possessor of riches. . . . He who possessed no property is now a man of wealth. . . . Jewels are fastened on the necks of slave girls. . . . The children of princes are dashed against walls."

In the Middle Kingdom, when order was restored by a centralized government from Thebes, the new era

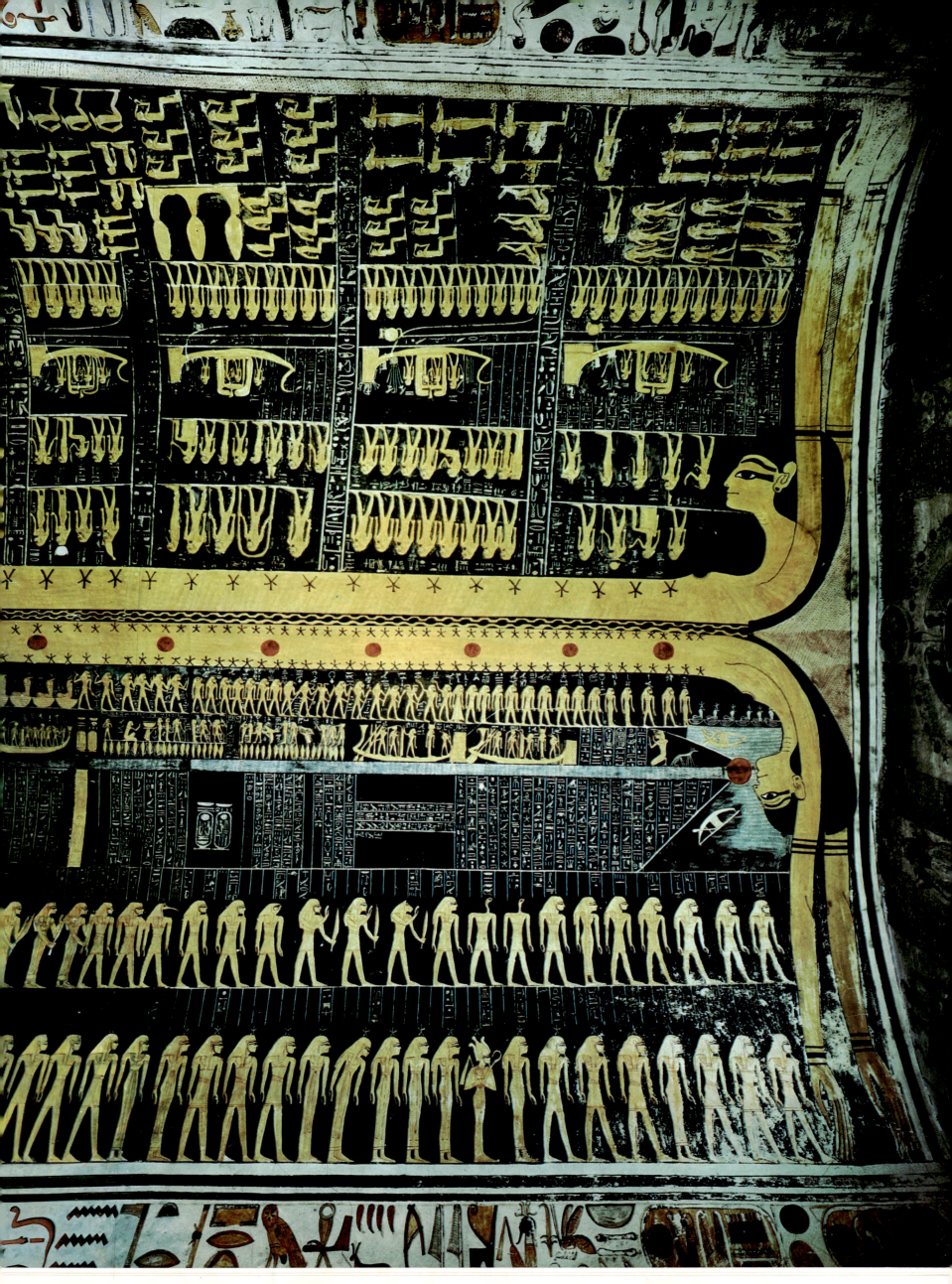

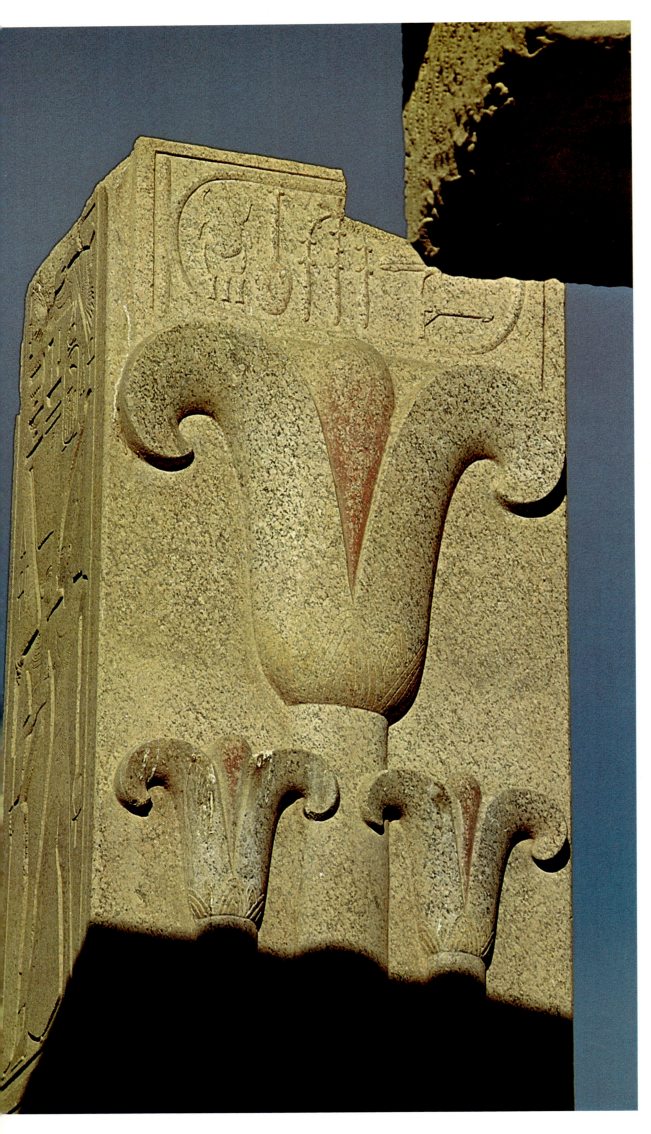

Symbols bloom in the garden of the gods

"Hail to you, Field of Offerings!" said those who walked in the temple courtyard. The only area of the temple open to the public, it was a place where offerings were deposited. Some were for the gods and some were for the dead. Other symbolic offerings appeared on the columns that towered like giant plants in the stone-floor field.

"Lilies," representing produce of the southern valley (Upper Egypt), grow from a pillar in the Temple of Amun-Re at Karnak (left). Papyrus flowers open atop columns of the temple colonnade at Luxor (right). Papyrus of the northern marshes symbolized Lower Egypt.

Ramses II, who completed the colonnade, sits before it on a throne, a symbolically tiny female relative below his elbow. He wears the double crown of the two Egypts and the uraeus cobra for the goddess of kingship. It came to symbolize the power of the pharaoh.

Inscriptions on the 52-foot columns, many of them too high for people in the courtyard to read, were instructions to the gods, who presumably could see them—and learn from human beings.

Another lesson tops the floral pillar (left). The name of Thutmose III is attached to the flower "at the very junction of heaven and earth." The pharaoh's name is in a cartouche. Once that symbol was circular, representing the sun and its heavenly realm. Stretched to an oval to enclose the royal name, it proclaims to the gods on high that the pharaoh reigns over "all that the sun encircles."

Overleaf: Tribute for a god "Great of Awe"

Ruins of the Temple of Amun-Re, largest columnar structure ever built, shimmer in the waters of its sacred lake at Karnak. Probably begun during the Middle Kingdom, the shrine was still being enhanced in the Ptolemaic Dynasty some 2,000 years later. Miles of painted reliefs covered the walls of the temple, which was 1,200 feet long. Its interior glowed with color: blue ceiling flecked with yellow stars, columns green, obelisks red, floors black, and walls white.

Etched in sky and water are, from left to right, remains of the monumental pylons leading to the courtyards; jagged remnants of the hypostyle hall; a 64-foot obelisk erected by Thutmose I, and a 97-foot one sponsored by his daughter Queen Hatshepsut.

The sacred lake provided holy water for priestly ablutions and rituals. The god's bark floated here on festival days. Symbolically, the lake recalled the fearful primeval flood "before men existed, before gods were born."

Reaching "to the height of heaven"

A field of columns thrusts to the sky in the hypostyle hall of Amun-Re's temple at Karnak. A colossal pharaoh stands nearby, his queen between his feet. In this fabulous world of giant metaphors, the hall is a field where dramas of creation take place. Here, say the tracts, the barley stands 7 feet high, the wheat 12 feet, and there are spirits of the afterlife tall enough to reap the great crops.

The real statistics sound awesome enough: The hall is 330 feet long and 170 feet wide, covering an area of about 56,000 square feet—big enough to hold the Cathedral of Notre Dame of Paris. The 12 tallest columns, each 79 feet high and 12 feet in diameter, raised the roofing slabs of the central nave above the level of other columns. This allowed light and air to enter through rows of stone-grilled clerestory windows, such as the one here. A total of 134 pillars supported the hypostyle hall.

The 32-foot statue in the courtyard stands as the "Unknown Pharaoh" while experts debate whether he is Ramses II and the miniaturized queen Nefertari. Some say he is Pinedjem, priest turned pharaoh, who put his name on a predecessor's sculpture.

Overleaf: Walls that tell royal tales

Great deeds of Ramses III emblazon his mortuary temple at Medinet Habu. Attendants with plumed sunshades and an incense burner lead a regal procession. In life, the pharaoh thus paraded here "to behold his father Amun-Re" on feast days. In death, the pharaoh still parades the stone. On the pylon beyond, he hunts the wild ass and antelope of the desert and (below this scene) the wild bull of the marsh. Archers guard him as, daringly poised on the tongue tree of his chariot, he drives his spear into his third kill of the hunt. Birds and fish dart in the papyrus thicket where the bulls fled for refuge. Such realistic scenes, by proclaiming the pharaoh's might, helped protect the temple, itself a refuge for Ramses after his death.

A mystic menagerie of beastly gods

Egyptians cherished animals and even mummified those deemed sacred. The cat portrayed Bastet, goddess of happiness. The pet *miu*—house cat—led a life blessed by Bastet. And when a miu died, its owners shaved eyebrows in mourning.

The falcon, sky-god image of mighty Horus, soared as the sign of the pharaoh. The stylized plumes and cobra-prowed uraeus of the falcon's crown join bird and serpent, symbols for the union of kingship and divinity.

Beast and man merge in the ram-headed god Harsaphes—"He who is on his lake." Name and image link the god to fertility, which popular notions associated with water and the virility of male sheep.

The hippo, here adorned with plants of its habitat, may have symbolized the struggle against the evil god Seth. Hippos were also sacred to Taueret, divine midwife and goddess of pregnant women.

The mongoose, here in bronze as a temple offering, was revered in some areas as a snake-killer but was hated for eating crocodile eggs in places where that animal was worshiped. The crocodile, as the ferocious god Sobek, wears ram's horns—and Maat's ostrich plumes, which show Sobek's link with order.

"Serve the god that he do the same for you"

The epigram helps explain why pharaohs took care of the gods. Rituals were performed in reality and in temple reliefs such as these. Amun-Re (opposite) gets clean clothes, and hieroglyphs record the helpful pharaoh's pun: "I have come not to dismantle the godly mantle . . . but to rehabilitate the godly habiliments."
The pharaoh (above) delivers a trayful of round bread, roast fowl, grapes, figs, and a pomegranate. As he perfumes another feast (left), incense pellets defy gravity to make a pleasing pattern. Wine jugs stand between four altar pedestals holding food offerings that include ducks and haunches of beef. Amun-Re, thus coaxed to give "all life," obligingly replies, "I have given you all that is splendid."

Overleaf: A cruise for father Amun

"Pharaoh conveys him who begot him," decrees another ritual performed by the ruler to honor his father the god. On the wall of a shrine in the Temple of Amun-Re at Karnak, a pharaoh obeys. Carrying an incense burner, he leads priests who bear a sacred bark. Its ram-headed prow and stern mark it as ancient Amun's. In processions, the statue of the god was taken from the temple and placed amidships in the bark. The shrine is hard to see on the wall, as it would be to watchers. Fine linen enwrapped the shrine, concealing the god who began as Amun, "the hidden one."

183

"A procession will be made for you"

A fine funeral was something to live for, if you were an Egyptian who could afford the high cost of dying in style. The laments of family and friends were led by professional mourners who shrieked, sprinkled dust on their heads, and tore their clothes. These weeping women, lamenting that their "great shepherd is gone," mourn eternally on the wall of the tomb of Ramose, a vizier of the New Kingdom.

In his procession, moving men (below) bear furniture for after-living rooms. Four carry chests that probably would have contained clothing; their shape reproduces the outline of an Upper Egypt shrine. One man clutches a walking stick, another totes a pair of white sandals.

Next come a pair burdened by a bed with bedding and headrest; they also carry a checkered bag and a fan. Speaking via the hieroglyphs between them, the rear man impatiently tells the one in front, "Get a move on! Stir your stumps!"

In Thebes, where Ramose was entombed, the participants in the funeral boarded ships on the east bank and disembarked on the west bank, along with the bier, the body, and the goods needed for a happy afterlife. The procession of wailing mourners headed for the city of the dead, the necropolis where tombs and mortuary temples awaited.

A typically mystic anagram tells why mourners cry. The sun god, who wept at his own funeral, explained, "That is how humans [romi] came into being—as the humors [rimi] which came forth from my Eye."

Overleaf: Last journey—"the silent land"

Mortuary temples and tombs emerge from the sand and stone of Deir el Bahri at the necropolis of Thebes. To Egyptian eyes, the setting sun buried itself each day in these 1,000-foot cliffs and, in mystical imitation, so at death did the royal family and nobility. The temple of Queen Hatshepsut—its three tiers a monument to endurance—reigns over the city of the dead. Though often depicted as a kilted, bearded man, she did rule in her own right. She took over from her male co-regent. After some 20 years in power, she died. Her nephew-stepson Thutmose III succeeded her, toppling her statues and effacing her name. But her memory still defies him.

She had a tomb in the Valley of the Kings, just beyond these cliffs. There New Kingdom pharaohs sunk tombs into the heart of a mountain, trying—usually in vain—to thwart thieves. Hatshepsut's burial chamber, 320 feet down into the rock, was among those robbed in antiquity.

"He who is yonder shall be a living god"

Like a window that opens to both life and afterlife, the wall of an artisan's tomb shows the double vision of Egyptian religion. Though the scenes portray life in paradise, they also give us a glance at a real landscape and its three seasons. Viewing from the bottom up, we see the wavy-lined Nile in flood, shrubs on the west bank, fruit trees on the east. In the next two seasonal registers, the deceased Sennedjem and his wife toil, wearing festive white, in the Egypt-like "Fields of the Blessed." They plow and seed (from right to left), pull flax, and (upper) take the grain of harvest. Each season had four 30-day months, for a 360-day year. The remaining five days became holidays for honoring gods depicted in the next register: Re, Osiris, Ptah, and two lesser deities; the couple kneels before them.

Atop all, Re in his bark is adored on New Year's day—around summer solstice—by sacred baboons. (Egyptians thought that baboons made such commotion at sunrise that they must have worshiped Re.) Inscriptions promise that Sennedjem will have an infinity of New Year's days.

If he tired of working in the fields, he had substitute figures called *ushabtis* or "answerers." A ushabti responded "Here I am!" when the deceased was summoned for labor. The figures here span dynasties and show changes in style; their inscriptions label them farm workers. A wealthy dead man would have one for each day of the year.

You will live again forever

The embalmer uttered this promise as he did his sacred work, leaving for posterity, if not eternity, that most fascinating of all relics: the mummy.

Some, such as the mummy of Ramses II (opposite), tell us tales. His X-rays showed he had eaten rough grains that had worn down his teeth, had gum disease and blackheads—and endured cold feet because of poor circulation. Long before his time, mummification had evolved from royal rite to civil right. But you got what you paid for. And the poor often got little more than burial in the sand.

Embalmings began with removal of organs that would decay. They usually were put into canopic jars (below), so called after a city where a god was worshiped in jar-like form. They were filled by a code linking each stopper-head to an organ: jackal, stomach; baboon, lungs; falcon, intestines; human, liver. The heads invoked Horus's protective sons.

The heart, as the site of intelligence, was blessed with a scarab, which Anubis the funerary god seeks (right) in a tomb painting. A hook put up the nose yanked out the worthless brain. The body was packed in salts, dried until leathery, and wrapped in some 20 layers of linen.

Change in a Changeless Land

Edna R. Russmann

You rise in perfection on the horizon of the sky,
Living Aten, who started life.
Whenever you are risen upon the eastern horizon
You fill every land with your perfection. . . .
You have made a far-off heaven in which to rise. . . .
Yet you are alone.

Thus, according to the inscriptions, Akhenaten, king of Egypt some 1,350 years before the birth of Christ, hymned his praises to the sun. This extraordinary man, perhaps physically deformed, husband to one of the most famous beauties in history, has been hailed as the inventor of monotheism—the worship of a single, all-powerful god. But, as we will see, Akhenaten's god was not entirely new, nor was it quite the only god. And Akhenaten himself would become a prophet dishonored in his own land. His memory would be reviled, his very existence expunged from the record by later rulers. Official documents would refer to him, if at all, as "that criminal." Nevertheless, one aspect of Akhenaten's ideas did survive, and would influence Egyptian culture for centuries—the arts.

Almost nothing is known about Akhenaten's childhood. He was the son of Amunhotep III and Queen Tiy. That much is certain. But where he grew up, how and when he acquired his revolutionary ideas—even the date of his birth—are questions that perhaps no amount of scholarly work will ever be able to resolve.

We do know that during the reign of Akhenaten's father Egypt basked in a golden age of power and prosperity. The court of Amunhotep III must have been as rich and cosmopolitan as any the world had yet seen. Such a court would have glittered with wealth and ideas from every quarter. Amunhotep's harem, for example, included even an Asiatic princess who, along with the customary gold and jewels, brought a retinue that included 316 ladies-in-waiting.

As for the idea of a sun god, Egyptians had worshiped Re in his human and animal forms since earliest times. From the beginning of the 18th Dynasty the

"Their arms are lifted in praise at your rising"

Words from the "Hymn to the Aten," Akhenaten's prayer to the sun, echo a scene of royal piety on a tablet (opposite) found at Amarna. Akhenaten and his queen, Nefertiti, pray before flower-laden stands, offering libations to the solar divinity that ruled over Egypt during their reign. The rays end in little hands that accept the offerings and, in turn, dangle before the royal couple symbols signifying "life." The king's breast bears the sun-god's name in cartouches. Fluid, curving lines and exaggerated physical features typify early Amarna art. Offering tables laden with meat, bread, and wine (left) represent a scene from the Great Temple at Amarna. About 3,000 such tables, placed row upon row in the compound, bore gifts to the sun.

importance of the sun itself, as the shining disk—or *Aten*—that traveled the heavens, had taken on a power of its own. People had begun to worship it, while the king, as ruler, had become identified with it. Amunhotep III himself was called "the dazzling sun disk."

From the beginning of his reign Akhenaten paid homage to the sun. A few early monuments show that at first he represented his deity in a traditional form—as a falcon-headed man. During these years he allowed other gods to coexist, and even continued to use the name he had been given as a child, Amunhotep, "Amun is pleased." By our numbering, he was Amunhotep IV. Only in the fifth or sixth year of his reign did he change his name to Akhenaten—"The Effective Spirit of the Aten." By then he had come to believe that there was no god but the sun, and that it took the form of the Aten, the radiant disk by whose light man lives.

Other gods—especially the state god, Amun—fell into eclipse. Some of their statues were smashed, their names chiseled away. Amun's great temple at Karnak was closed. So impassioned was the campaign against the state god that even the name of Akhenaten's father suffered mutilation because of its reference to Amun. Such was Akhenaten's "heresy."

To represent his deity, Akhenaten devised a hieroglyph-like symbol—a disk with rays of light ending in little hands. He created for it a new worship that took place, not in temple sanctuaries, but in the open—in large courtyards filled with altars and offering stands. No statues were carved of the Aten; it simply was present everywhere, shining down upon Akhenaten and his wife and daughters as they celebrated its rites.

Worship of the Aten was a public spectacle, with chariot processions to the temple, offerings heaped upon rows of altars, and crowds of followers lined up according to rank. But only the royal family actually took part in the services, and only the royal family received the blessings of the disk's many hands. The cult of the Aten was essentially a dialogue between Akhenaten and the disk, his divine father. Akhenaten even

had his own priests. Mortals could worship only him.

In exalting himself so far above mankind, Akhenaten elevated his family as well. His wife Nefertiti—"fair of face . . . mistress of happiness"—and their six daughters became far more prominent in public appearances than female and junior royalty had ever been. They also shared the spotlight in sculptures that portray their affectionate home life in charming detail—the girls swarming over their parents' laps.

The intimate nature of many scenes showing the royal family, and their evident fondness for one another, should not obscure from us their divine stature. Their affection also had a religious function. Akhenaten seems to have used the Egyptian love of family, and the tendency to endow nearly every god with a wife and child, to suggest a "Holy Family" of his own. It may be that Akhenaten intended the children and their mother to supply, in the new religion, the warmth and tenderness that the Aten so conspicuously lacked.

At about the time he changed his name to Akhenaten, the king journeyed to a place on the east bank of the Nile midway between Memphis and Thebes. Here he found virgin territory, a sandy plain hemmed by desert hills and cliffs. It was barren land that belonged, he tells us, to no god or goddess, nor to any prince or princess or any man. Here he founded a new city, marking its boundaries with huge stelae cut into the cliffs. On the stelae he named the temples and palaces he intended to build, and described the tombs he would carve for himself and his followers. He vowed he would be buried nowhere else.

Akhenaten called his city Akhetaten—"The Horizon of the Aten." We know the site as Amarna—or Tell el-Amarna—and it has given its name to the entire period of his reign. Those who travel to Amarna today find the same unproductive waste Akhenaten first saw, strangely empty and desolate. But the foundations of huge temples, palaces, and villas now lie under the drifting sand, all that remains of a city erected almost

overnight—and abandoned nearly as quickly after its founder's death. The royal tomb is a shattered wreck. Akhenaten probably kept his promise to be buried there. Because his mummy has not been found, we may never know. But Amarna was Akhenaten's home for the rest of his life; from Aten's city he sought to spread his ideas throughout the Egyptian empire.

The extent to which the new Aten cult touched the lives of the people is difficult to tell. Outside of Amarna, few records of Akhenaten's reign survive. Those that do are inconclusive. But when the king moved against the temples of the old gods, he must have given the country a jolt. If so, there is no trace of open resistance or revolt as long as he lived.

Interfering with temple rites may not have had much effect on the ordinary person. Egyptian ritual had always been mostly the business of priests performing their duties privately, in sanctuaries from which the public was barred. The Aten cult probably had little popular appeal, and certainly the people of Egypt must have found it hard to accept this god with no face, no personality, and no richness of myth or superstition. The people appear to have done what they had always done: offered their prayers to the humble gods, the homely little spirits who presided over practical matters like warding off snakes and scorpions and protecting women in childbirth. These household gods had no temples to lose, but they did hold people's hearts.

Whether or not Akhenaten actually wrote the sun hymn, he must certainly have been involved in the modernization of the written language that took place during his reign. He may also have had his own ideas about music. Unlike other gods, the Aten was serenaded by string ensembles that had previously performed at banquets. Troupes of foreign musicians were among them, some playing the giant lyre, an eastern instrument known in Egypt only during this time. Even the orchestras reflected the topsy-turviness of the new order. Male musicians now played certain women's instruments, like the boat-shaped harp, while women danced to the warlike trumpet.

But the innovations most visible to us, and in which we can most clearly see his personal intervention, lay in the visual arts—statuary, relief, painting. It may seem strange that a man so fanatically involved with restructuring the religion of his time should rethink the arts as well. It would probably not have occurred to Akhenaten to do otherwise. Every aspect of Egyptian life was permeated—had been formed—by religious belief. Every expression of what we today call art was, in a real sense, a religious expression. Ancient Egyptians had no word for "art," nor would they have understood our use of the term. The individual expected to live forever in human form through statues and other representations in his tomb. These images were far more potent than mere symbols. In a magical way, they *were* the being represented. We know of many cases in which posthumous revenge was taken by smashing a person's statue—or by simply breaking off its nose, so that he could no longer "breathe." When Akhenaten ordered the images of Amun destroyed, he may have intended, quite literally, to kill the rival god.

The inherently religious nature of Egyptian art imposed a conservatism that, to us, seems one of its main characteristics. But we must remember that this conservatism would not have been perceived as a restriction by the artist. A deliberate, conscious resistance to change was as deeply ingrained in ancient Egyptians as their hope that the sun would rise every morning. By their unchanging worship of the gods, they sought to maintain the pattern of the universe. The only thing wrong with life was its impermanence. Human life should—must—be made to go on forever. Stone was imperishable; wood and bronze, in that dry climate, nearly so. By means of his image, god, king, or mortal could last forever. Eternity was perhaps the most important single determinant of Egyptian art.

The rules of this art were laid down early. During the first three dynasties, from about 3100 to 2600 B.C.,

motifs and themes going back to prehistoric times were conventionalized—the human figure, the lordly animals including the lion and the falcon, and such evil ones as the hippopotamus and the crocodile. By the time of Cheops, the important artistic conventions had been decided upon. Almost all of them served to enhance solidity, clarity, harmony, balance. These criteria, not technical limitations, led Egyptian sculptors to leave a stone fill between the limbs of a statue so that it would be less vulnerable to breakage.

These rules endowed the human body with an ideal set of proportions, and determined that a standing man should be shown with the left leg forward, but with the weight comfortably and equally distributed on both feet. They dictated that the fist, whether holding an object or empty, should be clenched, so that the forearm muscles are visible, but not painfully tense.

The Egyptian sculptor could be a master at rendering an individual face. We see a few superb examples from Cheops's time. But individuality, alas, is impermanent. Far more prudent to make the face as idealized as the body, to eliminate any signs of age, illness, or care.

Carved and painted reliefs on tomb and temple walls presented special problems. Here it was necessary to show scenes of activity, often involving several figures, animals, and equipment. It was most important that there be no doubt as to what was going on. Short hieroglyphic statements explain the action, but no more describe the scenes than the scenes illustrate the writing. Egyptian writing and representation were part of each other to an extent that was possible only because the writing itself consisted of pictures. At about the time of the First Dynasty, the figures as well as the hieroglyphs had settled into orderly rows—registers, they are called, each with its base line. There is no perspective, no distance. Simply the surface along which the eye travels to "read" the design.

Ideals of clarity and comprehensibility governed the human form as well: A face in profile shows the eye frontally, its most important view; both shoulders are

The pursuit of a different vision

The dawn of a new religion brought a flowering of realism to ancient Egyptian art. Akhenaten's artists, seeking to "humanize" the abstract Aten, discarded old conventions and adopted new ones. Right and left feet—and hands—became clearly differentiated for the first time. Children began to look, and act, like children, not small-scale adults. Members of the king's family now were portrayed in informal poses—as in the reliefs of a princess dining on duck and one of the court ladies kissing a royal child.

seen, no matter what the position of the arms; both arms are visible, even when one is theoretically behind the body; hips and legs are drawn in profile, but the navel is also depicted because it is there. Only since the Greeks taught us to look at art the way we look at nature have these conventions come to seem in any way unnatural. The method is so logical and consistent, the transitions from one angle to another so gracefully worked out, that only an occasional awkwardness reminds us that we are looking, not at the imitation of a figure, but at the *idea* of one.

Every aspect of the artist's training and work helped reinforce his conservatism. He began as an apprentice, doing simple tasks. Because professions tended to run in families, he might well be introduced to his future trade while still a toddler, playing about his father's workshop. But the shop did not belong to his father. The artist was always in the service of a king, a temple, or a leading citizen. He did not choose his project; he did not own the materials he manipulated. In most cases, he probably did not even work on a single piece from start to finish.

The sculptor worked almost exclusively with stone tools, pounding and bruising away the excess, rubbing with abrasives to create the fine details and the final polish. Such a slow, laborious process could be made efficient only by using large numbers of less skilled workmen to prepare and rough out the stone. More highly skilled workers handled the advanced stages. The chief of the shop was a supervisor as much as he was a craftsman; his responsibilities included training

After the battle, the post mortem

Gory tokens of triumph—severed hands of slain enemies—pile up to be tallied and presented to the glory of the pharaoh. Inscriptions surrounding this detail from murals of Ramses III's second Libyan war put the trophy count at 2,175; living captives numbered another 2,052 (including 558 females). The traditional review might take place on the battlefield, with the pharaoh watching from his chariot, or, as here, from a rostrum.

In motifs and language of their battle monuments Egypt's warrior kings copied freely from their predecessors, altering only details and—of course—the star. Prisoners paraded before the pharaoh come "bound like fowl," bent in obeisance. Those below: Nubians in a frieze at Abu Simbel. Slavery awaited most captives. Relief (opposite) enacts a bloody ceremony of ancient origin requiring the king to sacrifice foes to Amun. Ramses II grasps the selected victims and ritually smites them with a mace.

Booty, the beauty of battle, included chariots, horses, asses, herds of cattle, weapons, gold, and other valuables of the vanquished that could be taken back home. Plunder enriched the estate of Amun, the king's coffers, and soldiers who showed special valor in the campaign. At the review of the spoils, a victor claimed a share based on the number of hands he put in the pile, proof of enemies killed. Fruits of incidental pillage of a downed village—food, wine, facilities for fun— strewed fringe benefits on the soldiers. What they seized was what they got.

"Let me tell you the woes of the soldier"

"He is called up for Syria. He may not
rest. There are no clothes, no sandals.
The weapons of war are assembled. . . ."
For the infantryman new wars, old woes.
His life had changed little since these
40 model spearmen marched into the
tomb of a nomarch, ruler of a nome,
in the strife-torn Middle Kingdom.

 Frequent wars of the empire needed
personnel trained and ready. Chariots,
each manned by driver and a fighter,
paced a more sophisticated warfare.
But most soldiers—bowmen, axmen,
spearmen—still traveled and fought on foot.
Spears, shorter than those shown above,
measured about three feet. Uniforms still
suited the climate: a short linen skirt,
a shield of raw cowhide with the spotted
hair outside, a helmet also of leather.
"His march is uphill through mountains.
He drinks water every third day. . . . His body
is ravaged by illness. The enemy comes,
surrounds him with missiles. . . . He is told:
'Quick, forward, valiant soldier!' "

237

"He has made his monuments like the stars of heaven"

Colossal quartet—all images of Ramses II—surveyed their first Nile sunrise 3,200 years ago. From Abu Simbel's rock bluff artisans hewed away what was not Ramses, leaving the four seated figures, 67 feet high and weighing 1,200 tons each. Their lips measure some three feet wide. One of the heads broke off from its torso centuries ago. In a niche above the portal of the temple stands a hawk-headed human figure crowned with a sun disk, depicting the pharaoh merged with Re-Harakhty. Not only absolute monarch, Ramses II was worshiped as a deity in his own time. Celebrating himself, he built grandiose monuments up and down the land.

"The All-Lord himself. . . . gave to me the land while I was in the egg; the great kissed the earth before me," boasts a Ramses inscription at the Abydos temple of his father, Seti I. Seti made Ramses co-regent while yet a child "that I may see his beauty while I live." He also gave him official duties and a harem. After warring at Seti's side in boyhood, Ramses as king and commander fought to maintain Egypt's Asian empire. "His might is in all lands, bringing for him multitudes of workmen from the captivity of his sword," says a notation on one of Ramses' Abu Simbel reliefs. With the relentless building activities of the Ramesside kings, particularly Ramses' namesake city, scholars have linked the Biblical oppression of Israel.

Multitudes of Ramses' workmen not only labored making sun-dried bricks but quarried the building blocks of previous pharaohs. Determined to eradicate relics of the hated Akhenaten, Ramses II left no Amarna stone unturned.

Abu Simbel, 180 miles above Aswan, had its own building material. The facade (above) fronts Ramses' Great Temple hewn 200 feet back into a sandstone monolith. Little damaged after a vigil of three millenniums, this and a smaller temple nearby were threatened in the 1960's by rising waters of the Aswan High Dam. In a massive international effort to save the priceless monuments, rescue crews cut the statues and their temples into huge blocks for transport to higher ground. Aware that vibration might break the crumbly sandstone—and leave scars on Ramses' faces—craftsmen hand-sawed the surfaces, then power-sawed from the back to finish cuts. Painstakingly reassembled, Ramses' "house of myriads of years" resumed its watch on the Nile.

"One long level beam . . . falls like fire"

Twice each year, rays of the rising sun penetrate to the sanctuary deep inside the great temple at Abu Simbel, flushing figures of the gods (left). A deified Ramses II shares the light with Amun of Thebes, at Ramses' right hand. Ptah of Memphis and Re-Harakhty of Heliopolis sit in shadow. The stone pedestal in the foreground served as a resting place for the sacred bark of the god. Four 30-foot pillars having features of Osiris, god of the underworld, flank each side of the hall (right).

Reliefs on the walls show Ramses the king offering cloth and incense before the bark of Ramses the god. One reads "incense to Ramses-meramen, may the incense come twice, may the perfume of Seth come, may the eye of Horus come . . . and the perfume of Nekhbet. . . ."

In the temple's new site the original orientation has been preserved. Maximum illumination by the dawning sun still occurs around October 20 and February 20. Egyptologist Louis Christophe believed the temple may have been planned so that sunshine would glorify Ramses' 30-year jubilee, about October 20, 1260 B.C.

240

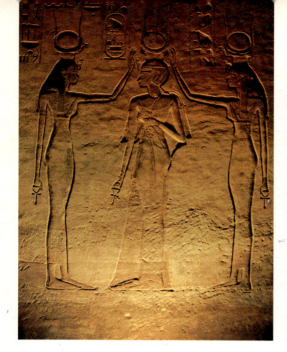

For the Great Royal Wife, a mansion

Before Nefertari's temple at Abu Simbel
Ramses II put the ultimate status symbol:
statues of his "Beautiful Companion"
as imposing as those of himself. Married
to Nefertari before he became king,
he gave her first place in a vast harem.
Twice cherished, each image of the queen
is flanked by two of Ramses (right).
As part of her high, feathered crown,
Nefertari wears the cow horns and solar
disk of the sky goddess Hathor.
The relief (above) pictures the queen's
divine coronation by Hathor and Isis.
A huge head of Hathor dominates a pillar
(below), one of six in the temple.
Nefertari's smaller temple complements
the Great Temple of Ramses at Abu Simbel.

"On every pillar . . . names of Ramses
and Nefertari 'coupled and inseparable,'"
wrote traveler Amelia Edwards. "We see
that the Queen was fair . . . the King was
in his prime. We divine the rest;
and the poetry of the place . . . is ours. . . .
a breath from the shores of old romance."

To speak of the dead, in the religion
of the ancient Egyptians, is to make them
live again. While such monumental stones
endure, inspiring awe and wonder in all
who see, speech is automatic. And the
people who raised them long ago seem to
move again to the rhythms of the Nile,
"given life, like Re, forever."

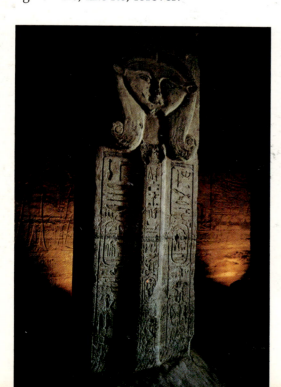

Across a span of 5,200 years, this overview of ancient history sketches events in Egypt against a backdrop of happenings in the rest of the world.

Dates in the chronology here—and throughout the book—are approximations. New archeological findings or fresh interpretations of old ones, along with new developments in dating methods, make for recurring revisions. And for all the ancient world, dates are so interdependent that a change in one can affect a number of others, domino-fashion. We have used those currently accepted by major authorities.

Problems arise too with the spelling of Egyptian names. The lack of vowels in hieroglyphic writing has already been touched on (page 143). But there can be bewildering turns. Some scholars argue, for example, that "Amun" should be spelled with a "u" when the stress falls on that vowel—as in the god A*mun*—but with an "e" when the stress is elsewhere—as in "Amen*hot*ep." Others disagree. In addition, scholars around the world have spelling conventions based on their own languages, and sometimes these show up in English translations of their works.

Further complications crop up in spellings based on Egyptian words from Babylonian tablets written in cuneiform, which does set down vowels. From this we get such forms as "Amanhatpi" instead of "Amunhotep." But experts argue that this derivation, from a foreign tongue, is no certain guide to ancient Egyptian usage.

Then there is the fact that Greek domination of Egypt for centuries brought indelible change. Greeks put a veneer of their words on people and gods and places. As a result, we are more familiar with Cheops than Khufu, Osiris and Isis than Usir and Aset, Memphis and Thebes than names long lost or obscure.

Modern Arabic pronunciation adds to the complexities. Archeological sites and place names are known by Arabic words that are difficult to transliterate in our Western alphabet. So one meets Idfu as well as Edfu, Saqqara and Sakkara, Qurna or Qurneh or Gurna.

Even among experts, no general agreement resolves such problems as those reviewed briefly above. We have tried, in this book, to conform to the simplest and the most common spelling.

VASE/COOK POT, CA 4750 B.C.

Egypt's Predynastic Period begins around 5200 B.C. Small bands of hunter-gatherers roam the Nile Valley. Herding and agriculture are known, but little practiced. Excavations of camps, cemeteries, and settlements have unearthed pottery, baskets, beads, stone tools, slate palettes for cosmetics. Pottery found near El Badari has given the name "Badarian" to one early culture.

POTTERY PIG, CA 5600 B.C.

Farms and farming villages expand in **Mesopotamia.** Mud bricks used in building. Wheat and barley established as staple crops; farmers have domesticated goats, sheep, cattle, and swine. Earliest evidence of the taming of pigs found in Turkey, where the pottery figure above was unearthed near Hacilar. First use of hammered copper for tools and ornaments occurs in Iraq, spreads throughout Mesopotamia, presumably by trade.

Agriculture develops in **China** and the valley of the **Indus River.**

Hunting-fishing cultures in **Europe** leave rock carvings and animal sculptures of stone and amber. In **Middle America,** after big game dies out, hunter-gatherers experiment with food plants—corn, beans, squash.

BIRD DEITY, CA 4000 B.C.

Farming takes over from a hunting-fishing way of life along the Nile. Towns, sometimes fortified, become established. Sailboats ply the Nile and explore Mediterranean shores. Fine flintwork and pottery with crosslined designs in white are made. People of late predynastic times develop a single culture archeologists call the Amratian, or Naqada I.

SUMERIAN STAMP SEAL, CA 3500 B.C.

Sumerian city-states come into existence along the Tigris and Euphrates rivers, centering around temples of mud brick. Work in copper becomes highly sophisticated. Impressions from stamp seals used as identification tags. They lead to cylinder seals, and eventually to the development of writing.

People of the **Danube River** basin produce skillful copperwork, and, by the end of this period, goldwork. Metalworking may have developed independently at several places in Europe not long after its beginnings in the Near East.

Megalithic—huge rough stone—tombs are erected in western **Europe.** They date from 4000 B.C., the oldest known stone structures.

GOLD ORNAMENT, DANUBE, CA 3500 B.C.

GERZEAN VASE, CA 3400 B.C.

Influences from outside the Nile Valley spark development of the Gerzean, or Naqada II, culture. Larger towns, rudimentary irrigation mark the change. Wattle-and-daub houses give way to rectangular structures of mud brick. Pottery shows new painting techniques, incised decoration, lug handles. Tombs become more elaborate; chambers, wall paintings are added.

SUMERIAN PICTOGRAPH TABLET, CA 3000 B.C.

Sumerian civilization climbs to new heights with invention of the cart wheel and the potter's wheel (and first mass-produced pottery). At the same time the first writing—pictographs—develops; earliest known use dates from about 3200 B.C. Pictographs and the wheel spread quickly to neighboring areas. Sumerians also devise the numbering system that would give us our 360-degree circle and our 60-minute hour.

Farmers in **China** cultivate rice, millet—and the silk moth.

In **Middle** and **South America,** nomadic hunter-gatherers settle into permanent villages, develop agriculture. People of the Peruvian Andes domesticate the llama. In **North America,** signs of a settlement appear in a sheltered site in the Illinois River Valley.

NARMER PALETTE, CA 3000 B.C.

FUNERARY STELA, CA 3000 B.C.

STEP PYRAMID, SAQQARA, CA 2650 B.C.

GREAT SPHINX, GIZA, CA 2550 B.C.

Separate political units—districts or provinces called "nomes"—begin to join forces. In time a single leader wins control of all nomes in Upper Egypt and achieves status as god-king. Unification with nomes of Lower Egypt is accomplished about 3050 B.C., and the pharaohs of Dynasty 1 rule all Egypt. The name of conquering King Narmer shows on a slate palette in an early form of hieroglyphs.

A new capital for the unified Egypt rises at Memphis. Royal and religious pomp and power grow as Dynasty 2 gains the throne. Pharaohs and noblemen build even more elaborate tombs. Egyptians devise an accurate stellar calendar, become expert at working copper and gold. Hieroglyphic writing, with many pictographic elements, decorates temples and tombs. A cursive form develops for writing on newly invented papyrus.

The Pyramid Age emerges in Egypt. Architect Imhotep builds a step pyramid for King Djoser of Dynasty 3. It stands as the world's first massive monument of hewn stone. Cult of the sun god Re flourishes at Heliopolis, stimulating the sciences of astronomy and mathematics.

Building of Bent Pyramid for King Snefru of Dynasty 4 ushers in construction of true pyramids. Cheops's great monument rises at Giza and shortly afterwards Chephren's with its guardian Sphinx. Egyptians war against Nubia and Libya, undertake trade expeditions in the Mediterranean. Old Kingdom reaches its zenith.

Sumerians usher in the Bronze Age, alloying copper first with arsenic, later with tin. Artistic skills and technology in bronze spread throughout the **Near East.** Sumerians also develop techniques for layering mud brick into solid, towering ziggurats—"mountains." Ceremonial stairways rise past intricate stepped terraces to temples at the top.

Large and complex semicircular structures of limestone blocks, perhaps the world's first stone temples, take shape on the Mediterranean island of Malta. "Fat lady" figurines found there may represent a mother goddess or fertility cult symbol—a central

Flourishing Sumerian city-states establish royal dynasties, reach populations as large as 50,000. Their cultural influence spreads across the **Near East.** Stone figurines and a bull-shaped vase found in Iran reflect a close relationship to the classic art of Sumer. Trade routes develop. Trading posts and towns are established in Palestine, Syria, and Anatolia—including the first settlement of Troy.

The horse is domesticated in southwestern **Asia** and the soybean in **China.** Earliest cultivation of cotton appears in the **Indus Valley**—and in **Peru.**

Pictographs come into use in

DETAIL FROM STANDARD OF UR, CA 2600 B.C.

Semitic peoples spread into **Mesopotamia** from the western deserts. Sumerian city-states (Uruk, Ur, and Kish) war against each other for dominance. Bureaucratic need to keep records leads to development of cuneiform writing. Royal cemetery at Ur sees burials of vast treasure, sacrificed retainers. Lyre player above ornaments a corner of an Ur

CUNEIFORM TABLET, EBLA, CA 2400 B.C.

Sumerian civilization soars with a highly organized political system, a complex religion, masterful achievements in art and architecture. Ur becomes the richest and most powerful city of all **Mesopotamia.** Rival Ebla shapes a Canaanite empire embracing Palestine and Syria. Recent Ebla finds yield 15,000 archival tablets; they are written in a cuneiform text that reflects a previously unknown Semitic language.

Indus Valley civilization flourishes. Sophisticated planned cities such as Mohenjo-Daro and Harappa have straight streets, buildings of fired brick, a sewer system. Water buffalo and yak are domesticated in **India** and **Tibet.**

Pottery making spreads from centers in **Ecuador** and **Mexico.**

STONEHENGE, CA 2600 B.C.

MALTESE FIGURINE, CA 3100 B.C.

BULL VASE FROM IRAN, CA 3000 B.C.

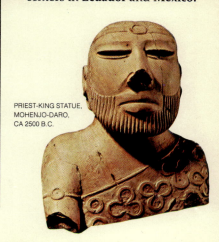

PRIEST-KING STATUE, MOHENJO-DARO, CA 2500 B.C.

feature of early religions across **Europe** and **Asia.** The example above is 19 inches tall.

Potters in **China** and **Japan** produce elaborately modeled and painted jars. Earliest pottery in the **Americas** appears in Ecuador and Colombia, with techniques and designs that some archeologists believe may have been brought by visitors from Japan.

northern **India** as the remarkable Harappan culture takes root along the Indus River.

mosaic depicting a victory celebration.

Early Minoan civilization flowers on **Crete.** Wheel comes into use in the **Indus Valley.**

Peoples of **Europe** construct megalithic chamber tombs, passage graves, and shrines such as England's Stonehenge. First stages of the latter, apparently laid out with astronomical observation, date to first half of third millennium B.C.

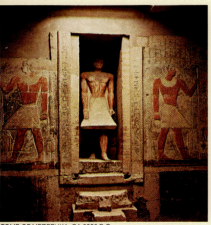
TOMB OF MERERUKA, CA 2350 B.C.

LADY KAWIT, CA 2040 B.C.

SHRINE OF SESOSTRIS I, KARNAK, CA 1950 B.C.

NOBLEMAN, 1790-1750 B.C.

Pharaohs begin calling themselves "Son of Re" and build elaborate sun temples. Pyramid Texts appear in royal tombs. High officials extol their own achievements in tombs nearby. Cedar from Lebanon and gold, ebony, incense, and ivory from Africa flow into Egypt.

Internal decay sets in during long reign of Pepy II, last major king of Dynasty 6. Power shifts to the nomarchs—rulers of the provinces. Egypt splinters.

Social and political chaos marks First Intermediate Period; tombs are ransacked, cultural traditions disrupted. Provinces engage in petty warfare against each other. Herakleopolitans restore order in the north, then Theban princes of Dynasty 11 reunite the country and initiate the Middle Kingdom. Thebes becomes the capital. Monumental building projects are revived, trade routes renewed. Egyptians begin to smelt bronze.

Powerful monarchs undertake large irrigation projects, intensify trade, build fortresses in the south. Egypt controls Nubia by the time of Sesostris III. He curbs nobles, helps rise of middle class based on trade, bureaucracy. Court and royal burials shift north to a site near Memphis, but Thebes remains a center of worship. Cultural splendor grows—pyramids at Dahshur, a shrine at Karnak, sculpture in the round.

Parade of pharaohs—some 50 in 150 years—marks Dynasty 13. At the same time western Delta secedes and 76 kings rule there as Dynasty 14. Nubia becomes independent. Decline of central government leads to the Second Intermediate Period. Hyksos—"chiefs of foreign lands"—arise in eastern Delta and set up Dynasties 15 and 16. They introduce the chariot and horse, and their influence spreads over all Egypt.

BRONZE HEAD OF SARGON (?), CA 2300 B.C.

GUDEA OF LAGASH, CA 2140 B.C.

CYCLADIC IDOL, CA 2000 B.C.

MINOAN "SNAKE GODDESS," 1600-1550 B.C.

Sumerian *Epic of Gilgamesh,* one of the world's oldest literary compositions, is compiled. Amorites of Arabia's desert and Elamites of Iran shatter Sumerian renaissance. Amorites rule from Babylon.

Pictographic writing develops in **China.**

Minoan civilization undergoes a

Hammurabi, great ruler of the first **Babylonian** empire, sets down his law code. Babylonians make strides in mathematics and astronomy. Indo-Europeans settle in Iran, eventually to form Persian empire. Scholars date Abraham's Biblical trek to Canaan and Egypt in this period.

Natural disasters—floods, mud

Sargon of Akkad, Semitic warrior-king, unifies **Mesopotamia,** founds an empire stretching from the Mediterranean to the Persian Gulf. But his empire falls around 2200 B.C. to the Guti, nomads of the Zagros Mountains. Mesopotamian city-states again become autonomous.

Farming spreads in northern and eastern **China;** hunter-gatherer culture still marks the south.

Hittite tribes filter into central **Turkey.** Skilled metalsmiths there fashion treasures of gold, silver, copper, and bronze and experiment with smelting iron.

In northern, central, and western **Europe** villagers cultivate wheat and barley, raise cattle and sheep. Farming people erect huge stone monuments in the Orkney Islands.

From ashes of the Akkadian empire, Gudea of Lagash revives southern **Mesopotamia,** sets stage for final resurgence of Sumer. Ur-Nammu becomes king of Sumer and Akkad, issues the first known law code, erects magnificent buildings—including the storied ziggurat at Ur.

In northern **China,** Hsia Dynasty is founded, based on slavery.

Minoan civilization on **Crete** builds planned cities with royal palaces, develops a writing system. Migrant "beaker people," named for their pottery, introduce copper and bronze to western and northern **Europe.** The wheel reaches the North Sea. Scandinavians first use skis.

Peruvians work designs in cotton textiles. Maize agriculture spreads through **Middle America.**

Native peoples of the **Great Lakes** and the Mississippi Valley hammer out copper tools. Ancestors of Eskimos reach Greenland.

meteoric rise on **Crete.** People of the Cyclades Islands in the Aegean make stylized statues and carvings of ivory. Their culture spans from 2600 to 1800 B.C. Mycenaeans advance into Greece from the north. At Avebury in England, builders raise one of the largest megalithic centers in **Europe.**

Pottery making and cultivation of maize take root in **Peru.** **North America's** earliest pottery appears on south Atlantic coast. Eskimo culture develops in Alaska.

volcanoes—spur collapse of **Indus** civilization; less advanced cultures of Aryan invaders are established in Bombay and Ganges regions.

Shang Dynasty rises in Hwang Ho Valley of **China.** Its warrior-landlord society is to last five centuries.

Advances in architecture and plumbing stand among achievements of **Minoan** civilization, now at its height. Multistoried palace at Knossos dominates a city of 80,000.

People of **Europe** become identifiable as Slavs, Teutons, Finns, and ancestors of Celts.

HATSHEPSUT, CA 1485 B.C.

BUST OF NEFERTITI, CA 1355 B.C.

ARTIST'S TOMB, CA 1150 B.C.

GOD TRIAD: HORUS, OSIRIS, ISIS, 874-850 B.C.

Theban princes expel the Hyksos, reunite Egypt. Dynasty 18 begins the New Kingdom and Egypt's golden imperial age. Warrior pharaohs extend Egypt's boundaries, embrace Palestine, Syria, Nubia. Tomb of Thutmose I becomes the first to be cut in the cliffs of the Valley of the Kings. Book of the Dead recorded on papyri, placed in tombs.

Amunhotep III reaps splendor of Egypt's empire; court life at Thebes is luxurious, cosmopolitan. His son Amunhotep IV defies powerful priests of Amun and proclaims a worship of the sun's disk, the Aten. He changes his name to Akhenaten, builds a new capital at Amarna, ushers in realistic art. His successors, including Tutankhamun, restore old ways. First Ramesside dynasty renews military activity abroad.

Ramses III, the last strong pharaoh, drives back invading Libyans and Sea Peoples. But Egypt sinks into a decline. Tomb robbery grows flagrant, workers strike for lack of rations, conspirators plot the king's assassination. By the end of Dynasty 20, the pharaoh, the high priest at Thebes, and the viceroy of Nubia share power. A procession of Ramesside rulers marks the close of the New Kingdom. Unrest of the Third Intermediate Period follows.

Pharaonic capital moves to the Delta; Amun's high priest rules a theocratic state from Thebes. Dynasties 22 and 23 see a joint reign by Libyan families that had become Egyptianized in the western Delta. The first Libyan pharaoh, Sheshonq I (the Shishak of the Bible), pillages Jerusalem. By end of Dynasty 23 the Delta is dividing into city-states. Sculptors in this period produce exquisite statuettes in metal.

The Mitanni form a new empire in northern **Mesopotamia.** Hittites maintain a flourishing iron industry. Alphabetic use of pictographs by Semitic people in the Sinai is possible forerunner of the Phoenician alphabet.
    Warlike Mycenaeans, established

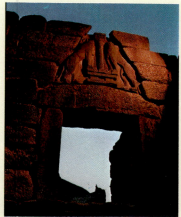

LION GATE, MYCENAE, CA 1250 B.C.

Iron Age brings advances to the Aegean, Syria, and Palestine. Hebrews establish monotheism in Canaan, make Saul their first king. Phoenicians become a force in Syria and Lebanon.
    In **India,** rice farming develops, Hindu Rig Veda hymns are set down.
    Mycenaeans conquer Troy, then

PHOENICIAN NORA STONE, 9TH CENTURY B.C.

MYCENAEAN MASK, CA 1550 B.C.

Moses leads Hebrews from Egypt in the Biblical Exodus. Hittite empire collapses, conquered by invaders from Thrace. Use of iron becomes common in the **Near East.**
    Mycenaean civilization peaks;

WARRIOR VASE, MYCENAE, 12TH CENTURY B.C.

Phoenicians build trading colonies, such as Carthage and Cadiz, around the **Mediterranean.** Their script is adopted by the Greeks, in turn to find its way into our alphabet. David makes Jerusalem his capital; his successor, Solomon, builds the Templ
    Ancestor worship, with elaborate ritual, reaches a peak in **China.**
    Etruscans settle in **Italy.** Crete and Greece endure a period of darkness, accompanied by major migrations.
    Platforms of earth or stone for use as ceremonial centers are built in **Mexico** and **Peru.** Adena culture, with elaborate burials, centers in **Ohio Valley.**

in citadels in mainland **Greece,** move into Crete, overthrow Minoans. Mycenaean rulers are interred with gold treasures in shaft graves.
    Bronze Age expands in **Europe.** New technology prompts improved designs in jewelry, tools, weapons.
    Aryans spread Sanskrit language and many elements of Hindu religion in **India.** Shang Dynasty spurs **Chinese** civilization; cities emerge as trade centers, agrarian fiefdoms shape the countryside. High art develops in bronze.
    Farm-village cultures in **Middle America** grow more complex; large communities develop in **Peru.**

OWL-SHAPED BRONZE WINE VESSEL, CHINA, 11TH CENTURY B.C.

it dominates all **Greece;** its trade covers the eastern Mediterranean.
    Aryan caste system evolves in **India.** Shang Dynasty founds its capital near An-yang in **China.**

are overthrown by Indo-European northerners swarming down the Peloponnesian Peninsula.
    Olmec civilization appears in **Middle America.** Tlatilco villagers in the area of present-day Mexico City model elaborate figurines for use in burials.

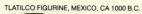

TLATILCO FIGURINE, MEXICO, CA 1000 B.C.

OLMEC HEAD, 1000-850 B.C.

MENTUEMHAT, CA 660 B.C.

BRONZE CAT, CA 600 B.C.

LION VESSEL, 525-404 B.C.

HEAD OF WESIRWER, CA 360 B.C.

Nubians from Kush, under King Piankhy, conquer Egypt. Kushite rule ends with Assyrian conquest and sack of Memphis and Thebes. Saite Dynasty reunites Egypt and rebuilds its power and prestige, but Pharaoh Neko II's attempt to regain its empire is defeated by Nebuchadnezzar II. The Iron Age and camel reach Egypt in this period. Mentuemhat has a long tenure as a powerful governor of Upper Egypt.

Cities of the Delta thrive under Saite restoration of Egypt. One of them, Bubastis, is the cult city of the goddess Bastet whose sacred animal is a cat. Neko II sanctions an attempt to build a canal from the Nile to the Red Sea, sends an expedition to sail around Africa. Streams of immigrants—Greeks, Syrians, Hebrews—flow into Egypt. In 525 B.C. King Cambyses II of Persia adds Egypt to his empire.

Persian rulers adopt the trappings of the pharaohs and maintain Egyptian culture. Egypt's legal system is codified. But revolts break out, spurred by Greek victories against Persians such as that at Marathon. Finally in 404 B.C. the Egyptians throw off the Persian yoke.

Political turmoil and uncertainty mark rule of Egypt's last native kings. Persians again briefly gain control in 341 B.C. Their defeat in Asia by Alexander the Great leads to his whirlwind conquest of Egypt and establishment of dynasties under Macedonians and the Greek Ptolemies. Scholarship and trade flourish in Alexandria, their capital. It would boast a luxurious court, a university, and a library housing 400,000 scrolls.

"MONA LISA OF NIMRUD," 8TH CENTURY B.C.

Assyria reaches its pinnacle; Nimrud, one of its capitals, is rebuilt. But fall of the capital at Nineveh in 612 B.C. topples the nation. Mounted Scythians raid from their Black Sea home, join with Medes to bring down Assyria. **Babylon** climbs again into importance as an empire.

Etruscan civilization flourishes. Rome is founded (753 B.C.). Greece rises. First Olympic games take place, Homer's *Iliad* and *Odyssey* are written down. Celts emerge as a distinct people, spread ironworking through northern and central **Europe,** move into England.

Iron replaces bronze in **China.** Chou Dynasty struggles with rising challenge of rival warring states.

WARRIOR FRIEZE, PERSEPOLIS, 6TH-5TH CENTURIES B.C.

Nebuchadnezzar II takes over the fertile crescent of the **Near East.** He rebuilds Babylon, razes Jerusalem, carries Jews into captivity. Persians led by Cyrus the Great conquer **Babylonia.** Jews gain freedom. Darius I founds the Persian capital of Persepolis, extends Persian empire to the Indus.

Mahavira Jina rebels against **India**'s ritualistic religion, sets out the ascetic philosophy of Jainism. Teachings of Gautama Buddha begin Buddhism.

Etruscans expand in **Italy,** but in 509 B.C. rebelling Romans found the Roman republic. The Greek city-state of Athens expels a tyrant, Hipparchus, and creates a democracy.

China undergoes upheaval in a change from a slave to a feudal system. Lao Tzu forges Taoism; Confucius preaches his concepts.

ETRUSCAN SARCOPHAGUS SCULPTURE, CA 500 B.C.

Greeks, under leadership of Sparta, defeat Persian armies. Persians also gradually lose dominions in the **Near East, India.** Their liberal and brilliant civilization wanes.

Athens rises as a power. Golden Age of Pericles, named for the Athenian statesman, sees great works of literature, philosophy, and art and such immortals as Socrates, Hippocrates, Herodotus, Sophocles. Envy and hostility of other Greek states leads to Peloponnesian Wars.

PARTHENON, FINISHED 432 B.C.

Etruscan power ebbs. **Rome** firms independence, sets laws guaranteeing liberty, property, due process.

China slips into anarchy, a time of constantly warring states.

Olmec civilization in **Middle America** begins decline.

POT WITH SPOUT, PERU, 500-250 B.C.

Greek city-states jockey for supremacy. In 338 B.C. Philip II of Macedon subdues the quarreling Hellenes and adds **Greece** to the Macedonian empire. After his assassination, his son Alexander consolidates the inherited realm, sweeps on to defeat Persia, Syria, and Egypt, and marches as far as the Indus Valley. Hellenistic culture washes over **Asia Minor.**

Rome, now mistress of the Italian peninsula, builds on

ALEXANDER, THRACIAN COIN, 3RD CENTURY B.C.

traditions of the Etruscans—a sophisticated, exuberant, and civilized folk. Rampaging Celts, whom the Romans call Gauls, sack Rome in 387 B.C. but are driven back; the city is soon rebuilt.

Scythian culture reaches a peak in the **Ukraine.**

Chandragupta founds the first Indian empire. It spreads over **India** and parts of central Asia. The epic poems *Mahabharata* and *Ramayana* are set down.

Internal strife and attacks by nomads plague **China,** but rival rulers foster trade. "Golden Age" of Chinese philosophy blossoms.

Farm settlements begin in **North America.** Pottery appears in the southwest; coastal tribes of the northwest build plank houses.

TEMPLE OF HORUS, BEGUN 3RD CENTURY B.C.

ROSETTA STONE, CA 196 B.C.

TEMPLE OF HATHOR, DENDERA, BEGUN 110 B.C.

Egypt's periods and dynasties

The list includes the number of kings and some notable rulers. Dates are B.C. and—before 664—approximate.

Under Ptolemies, Greek influence pervades Egyptian art and culture. Ptolemy III introduces leap year into Egypt's calendar. Manetho, an Egyptian priest, groups the pharaohs into dynastic divisions. In Alexandria, Eratosthenes calculates earth's circumference, Euclid formulates fundamentals of plane geometry, Archimedes makes basic discoveries in science.

Ptolemaic Dynasty begins to fade. Egyptians riot over living costs, heavy taxes—there is even a tax on tax receipts! Trouble breaks out in Alexandria among Egyptians, Greeks, and Jews. Threatened by Syrian and Macedonian invaders, Ptolemies place Egypt under the protection of Rome. Rosetta Stone is inscribed to honor Ptolemy V.

Tax revolts, animosities between ethnic stocks and classes continue. Under Rome's protection, Egypt's independent status slips, Ptolemies' hold weakens. Cleopatra VII, last of the dynasty, works her wiles on Julius Caesar and Mark Antony, but Egypt still falls to Rome in 30 B.C. Emperor Augustus assumes attributes of the pharaohs. Rome builds temples in Egyptian style. Exquisite temple at Dendera, begun by Ptolemies, is finished by Romans.

Predynastic Period, 5200-3050
Early Dynastic Period
DYNASTY 1, 3050-2890
  Eight kings, including Narmer
  (Menes), Aha, Djer, Djet
DYNASTY 2, 2890-2686
  Six kings
Old Kingdom
DYNASTY 3, 2686-2613
  Five kings, including Djoser
DYNASTY 4, 2613-2494
  Six kings . . . Snefru, Cheops,
  Chephren, Mycerinus
DYNASTY 5, 2494-2345
  Nine kings . . . Userkaf, Unas
DYNASTY 6, 2345-2181
  About seven kings . . . Pepy I
DYNASTY 7, 2181-2173
  About nine kings
DYNASTY 8, 2173-2160
  About six kings
First Intermediate Period
DYNASTIES 9 & 10, 2160-2040
  About eight kings
DYNASTY 11, 2133-2040
  Five kings . . . Mentuhotep I
Middle Kingdom
DYNASTY 11, 2040-1991
  Three kings . . . Mentuhotep II
DYNASTY 12, 1991-1780
  Eight kings . . . Sesostris I
DYNASTY 13, 1780-1633
  About 50 kings
Second Intermediate Period
DYNASTY 14, 1786-1603
  Seventy-six kings
DYNASTIES 15 & 16, 1674-1558
  The Hyksos kings
DYNASTY 17, 1650-1558
  About 15 kings
New Kingdom
DYNASTY 18, 1558-1303
  Fourteen kings . . . Ahmose,
  Amunhotep I, Thutmose I,
  Thutmose II, Queen Hatshepsut,
  Thutmose III, Amunhotep III,
  Akhenaten, Smenkhkare,
  Tutankhamun, Horemheb
DYNASTY 19, 1303-1200
  Eight kings . . . Ramses I, Seti I,
  Ramses II, Merneptah, Seti II
DYNASTY 20, 1200-1069
  Ten kings . . . Ramses III
Third Intermediate Period
DYNASTY 21, 1069-945
  Six kings
DYNASTY 22, 945-715
  Eight Libyan kings . . . Sheshonq I
DYNASTY 23, 818-715
  Six Libyan kings
DYNASTY 24, 727-715
  Two kings
DYNASTY 25, 760-656
  Six Kushite kings . . . Piankhy
Saite Renaissance
DYNASTY 26, 664-525
  Six kings . . . Psamtik I
Late Dynastic
DYNASTY 27, 525-404
  Five Persian kings
DYNASTY 28, 404-398
  One king
DYNASTY 29, 398-378
  Five kings
DYNASTY 30, 378-341
  Three kings
DYNASTY 31, 341-330
  Three Persian kings
Alexander's Conquest, 332
Macedonian Domination, 332-304
Ptolemaic Dynasty, 304-30 Fourteen
  kings . . . Ptolemy I, Cleopatra VII.
Roman Conquest, 30

Warrior-horsemen from the steppes drive Scythians into the Crimea. Parthians weld a kingdom in **Iran.**
  In the Punic Wars, Carthage loses Sicily and Spain to **Rome** despite Hannibal's thrust across the Alps. Roman fleets sail the Mediterranean.

Maccabean revolt frees the Jews from **Syrian** rule; independent Jewish state is formed, 142 B.C.
  Roman legions engulf eastern **Mediterranean, Greece, Asia Minor.** Carthage falls. Romans adopt Greek forms in art, building, literature.

Political unrest and violence rack the **Roman** republic. Caesar, with Pompey and Crassus, forms the First Triumvirate. Caesar assassinated in 44 B.C. Rivalry among successors ends with Octavian (Augustus) becoming the first Roman emperor. Augustan Age witnesses the peak of Roman art, the literature of Cicero, Ovid, Virgil, Horace.

WINGED VICTORY, SAMOTHRACE, 200-190 B.C.

VENUS DE MILO, 2ND CENTURY B.C.

JULIUS CAESAR, 1ST CENTURY B.C.

Huns, nomadic warriors, grow powerful in **Mongolia.** Ch'in Shih Huang Ti unifies **China,** builds the Great Wall, standardizes weights and writing—and is buried with a life-size pottery army of 6,000.
  Forebears set stage for rise of Maya civilization in **Middle America.**

Chinese invent paper. Emperor Wu Ti of Han Dynasty develops the Silk Route to the West, revives art and literature.
  In **North America,** people of the Hopewell culture raise huge burial mounds, tap a vast trade network.

Waterwheel comes into use in Greece and the **Near East.** Parthians rule from Euphrates to Indus. Birth of Jesus ushers in Christian era.
  Architects in Mexico engineer the massive Pyramid of the Sun. Peruvian Indians weave some of the finest textiles of the **New World.**

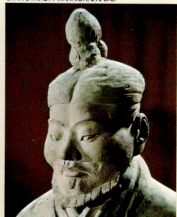

CH'IN DYNASTY WARRIOR, 210 B.C.

HOPEWELL HEAD, AFTER 100 B.C.

PERUVIAN EMBROIDERY, CA A.D. 1

Notes on the Authors

WILLIAM KELLY SIMPSON, editorial consultant for this book and author of the chapter on writing, is professor of Egyptology at Yale University and curator of Egyptian and ancient Near Eastern art at the Boston Museum of Fine Arts. He serves as a trustee of the American Research Center in Egypt and the American School of Classical Studies in Athens.

J. CARTER BROWN, who wrote the Foreword, is the director of the National Gallery of Art and a trustee of the National Geographic Society.

KARL W. BUTZER is professor of anthropology and geography at the University of Chicago and a professor in The Oriental Institute there. He is co-author of *Desert and River in Nubia* and author of many other books and articles.

VIRGINIA LEE DAVIS has taught courses in Egyptian art, history, mythology, and hieroglyphics at Harvard and Yale universities, and served as guest curator of Egyptian art at the New Orleans Museum of Art.

I. E. S. EDWARDS retired recently as Keeper of Egyptian Antiquities at the British Museum. He is joint editor of *The Cambridge Ancient History*. His many publications include authoritative studies on the pyramids and on Tutankhamun.

BARBARA MERTZ is the author of *Temples, Tombs and Hieroglyphs* and of *Red Land, Black Land*. She also draws on her background in archeology and history to write popular novels.

WILLIAM H. PECK is curator of ancient art at the Detroit Institute of Arts and adjunct professor of Egyptian art and archeology at Wayne State University.

EDNA R. RUSSMANN is assistant curator of the department of Egyptian art at the Metropolitan Museum of Art.

ANTHONY J. SPALINGER is lecturer of Egyptology in the department of Near Eastern languages and literatures at Yale University.

Acknowledgments

In the preparation of this volume we had the unstinting assistance of many individuals and organizations, and we gratefully acknowledge our indebtedness to them. Staff members of the Library of Congress and the National Geographic Society Library were generous with advice and cooperation. We would like also to thank particularly the following individuals:

Dr. Morsi Saad el-Din, director of information, Egyptian Ministry of Information and Culture; Dr. Dia Abou-Ghazi, Egyptian Museum, Cairo; Dr. and Mrs. Labib Habachi, Cairo; Dr. Ahmed Mousa, director of antiquities, Saqqara; and Ahmed Majahlawi, Cairo.

Dr. Lanny Bell, director of Chicago House at Luxor, and Mrs. Bell provided invaluable aid, as did May Trad, librarian of Chicago House; Abd El Hamid El Daly, Luxor; Said Higazi, director of antiquities, Luxor; Abdalla El Sayed M., director of the Luxor Museum; Sheikh M. Negdi, Qurna; and Jean Lauffray, of the Franco-Egyptian Center, Karnak.

Jennifer Moseley, London, gave liberal assistance, as did Carol Andrews of the British Museum; Dr. Jurgen Settgast and Jurgen Liepe of the Ägyptisches Museum, West Berlin; Frau Dr. Kischkewitz, Ägyptisches Museum, East Berlin; Bernard Bothmer and Richard Fazzini of the Brooklyn Museum; David W. Nasgowitz of The Oriental Institute; Dr. James B. Pritchard, University of Pennsylvania Museum; and Dr. Timothy Kendall, Boston Museum of Fine Arts.

We are grateful also for permission to reprint excerpts from *The Literature of Ancient Egypt*, edited by William Kelly Simpson © Yale University Press, New Haven, 1973.

Bibliography

In the extensive literature dealing with the civilization of ancient Egypt, we found many books helpful in preparing this volume. Those of a general nature with information applicable to most of the chapters included *Art in Ancient Egypt* by Cyril Aldred, London, 1968-72; *The Egyptians*, Cyril Aldred, New York, 1961; *A History of Egyptian Architecture*, Alexander Badawy, Berkeley, 1954-68; *Egypt and the Sudan*, Karl Baedeker, Leipzig, 1929; *Ancient Records of Egypt*, James H. Breasted, New York, 1906; *A History of Egypt*, James H. Breasted, New York, 1912; *The Cambridge Ancient History*, London, 1923-1977; *Living Architecture: Egyptian*, Jean-Louis de Cenival, New York, 1964; *Food: The Gift of Osiris*, William J. Darby and others, London, 1977; *The Egyptian Kingdoms*, A. Rosalie David, London, 1975; *Ancient Egyptian Paintings*, Nina M. Davies and Alan H. Gardiner, Chicago, 1936; *Description de l'Égypte*, France, Commission des Monuments d'Égypte, Paris, 1809-28; *Tutankhamen*, Christiane Desroches-Noblecourt, New York, 1963; *Tutankhamun: His Tomb and Its Treasures*, I. E. S. Edwards, New York, 1976; *Studies in Ancient Technology*, R. J. Forbes, Leiden, 1955-64; *Egypt of the Pharaohs*, Alan H. Gardiner, Oxford, 1961; *Magic and Medical Science in Ancient Egypt*, Paul Ghalioungui, London, 1963; *The Ancient Near East: A History*, William W. Hallo and William Kelly Simpson, New York, 1971; *The Legacy of Egypt*, J. R. Harris, Oxford, 1971; *The Scepter of Egypt*, William C. Hayes, Cambridge, Mass., 1953, 1959; *Technology in the Ancient World*, Henry Hodges, New York, 1970; *Ships of the Pharaohs*, Björn Landström, Garden City, N.Y., 1970; *Egypt*, Kurt Lange and Max Hirmer, London/New York, 1968; *Saqqara*, Jean-Philippe Lauer, New York, 1976.

Ancient Egyptian Materials and Industries, A. Lucas and J. R. Harris, London, 1962; *Egyptian Painting*, Arpag Mekhitarian, Geneva, 1954; *Temples, Tombs and Hieroglyphs*, Barbara Mertz, New York, 1964; *Art of Ancient Egypt*, Kazimierz Michalowski, New York, 1977; *Eternal Egypt*, Pierre Montet, New York, 1964; *The Splendor that was Egypt*, Margaret A. Murray, New York, 1963; *Egyptian Museum, Cairo*, Newsweek, New York, 1969; *Ancient Egyptian Art*, Eberhard Otto, New York, 1967; *Topographical Bibliography of Ancient Egyptian Hieroglyphic Texts, Reliefs, and Paintings*, Bertha Porter and Rosalind L. B. Moss, Oxford, 1927-64; *Dictionary of Egyptian Civilization*, Georges Posener, New York, 1962; *Ancient Near Eastern Texts Relating to the Old Testament*, James B. Pritchard, Princeton, 1969; *The Ancient Near East in Pictures*, James B. Pritchard, Princeton, 1969; *The Egyptians*, John Ruffle, Ithaca, N.Y., 1977; *Egyptian Architecture*, E. Baldwin Smith, New York/London, 1938; *The Art and Architecture of Ancient Egypt*, W. Stevenson Smith, Harmondsworth, Eng., 1958; *Treasures of Egyptian Art from the Cairo Museum*, E. L. B. Terrace and H. G. Fischer, Boston, 1970; *Painting, Sculpture, and Architecture of Ancient Egypt*, Wolfhart Westendorf, New York, 1968; *The Burden of Egypt*, John A. Wilson, Chicago, 1951; *The Art of Egypt*, Irmgard Woldering, New York, 1963; *Treasures of the Pharaohs*, Jean Yoyotte, Geneva, 1968.

For specialized study on particular chapters, we found these references helpful:

The Constant Lure *Narratives . . . in Egypt and Nubia*, G. B. Belzoni, London, 1820; *The Tomb of Tut-Ankh-Amen*, Howard Carter, New York, 1923; *Who Was Who in Egyptology*, Warren R. Dawson, London 1972; *Travels in Upper and Lower Egypt*, Vivant Denon, London, 1803; *The Rape of the Nile*, Brian Fagan, New York, 1975; *Egyptian Obelisks*, Henry H. Gorringe, New York, 1882; *The Discovery of Egypt*, Leslie Greener, London, 1966; *The Obelisks of Egypt*, Labib Habachi, New York, 1977; *Bonaparte in Egypt*, J. Christopher Herold, New York, 1962; *The History of Herodotus*, trans. by George Rawlinson, London/Toronto/New York, 1910; *The Great Belzoni*, Stanley Mayes, London, 1959; *Ten Years' Digging in Egypt*, W. M. Flinders Petrie, London, 1891; *A History of Egyptian Mummies*, Thomas J. Pettigrew, London, 1834; *A Description of the East and Some Other Countries*, Richard Pococke, London, 1743; *Egyptian Mummies*, G. Elliot Smith and Warren R. Dawson, London, 1924; *Signs and Wonders Upon Pharaoh*, John A. Wilson, Chicago, 1964; *Excavations at Deir el Bahri*, H. E. Winlock, New York, 1942.

The People of the River *Egypt to the End of the Old Kingdom*, Cyril Aldred, New York, 1976; *Early Hydraulic Civilization in Egypt*, Karl W. Butzer, Chicago, 1976; *The Prehistory of Africa*, J. Desmond Clark, New York, 1970; *Archaic Egypt*, Walter Emery, Baltimore, 1961; *Ancient Kingdoms of the Nile*, Walter A. Fairservis, Jr., New York, 1962; *Barrow, Pyramid, and Tomb*, Leslie V. Grinsell, London, 1975; *Most Ancient Egypt*, William C. Hayes, Chicago, 1965; "Stone-age Man on the Nile," Philip E. L. Smith in *Scientific American*, August, 1976; *Beyond History: The Methods of Prehistory*, Bruce G. Trigger, New York, 1968; "Egyptian Prehistory: Some New Concepts," Fred Wendorf and others in *Science*, Sept. 18, 1970.

Pyramids: Building for Eternity *The Pyramids of Egypt*, I. E. S. Edwards, New York, 1972; *The Pyramids*, Ahmed Fakhry, Chicago, 1961; *Egyptian Pyramids*, Leslie Grinsell, Gloucester, Eng., 1947; *The Pyramids and Sphinx*, Desmond Stewart, New York, 1971.

The Pleasures of Life *Jewels of the Pharaohs*, Cyril Aldred, London 1971; *Furniture in the Ancient World*, Hollis S. Baker, London, 1966; *Daily Life in Ancient Egypt*, Lionel Casson, New York, 1975; *Life in Ancient Egypt*, Adolf Erman, London, 1894; *The Ancient Egyptians*, Jill Kamil, Chester Springs, Pa., 1977; *Red Land, Black Land*, Barbara Mertz, New York, 1966; *The History of Musical Instruments*, Curt Sachs, New York, 1940; *The Daily Life of the Ancient Egyptians*, Nora Scott, Metropolitan Museum Bulletin, New York, Spring 1973; *Egyptian Jewellery*, Milada Vilímková, London, 1969; *Everyday Life in Ancient Egypt*, Jon Manchip White, London/New York, 1963; *Ancient Egyptian Jewellery*, Alix Wilkinson, London, 1971; *The Manners and Customs of the Ancient Egyptians*, J. Gardner Wilkinson, Boston, 1883; *Models of Daily Life in Ancient Egypt*, H. E. Winlock, Cambridge, Mass., 1955.

The Gift of Writing *Paper and Books in Ancient Egypt*, Jaroslav Černý, University College, London, 1947; *The Alphabet*, David Diringer, New York, 1968; *The Literature of the Ancient Egyptians*, Adolf Erman, trans. by A. H. Blackman, London 1927; *Egyptian Grammar*, Alan H. Gardiner, Oxford, 1957; *The Hekanakhte Papers*, T. G. H. James, New York, 1962; *Papyrus in Classical Antiquity*, Naphtali Lewis, Oxford, 1974; *Ancient Egyptian Literature*, Miriam Lichtheim, Berkeley, 1973, 1976; *The Literature of Ancient Egypt*, ed. by William Kelly Simpson, New Haven, 1973.

Pathways to the Gods *The Egyptian Book of the Dead*, E. A. Wallis Budge, London, 1895; *Thebes*, Jean Capart, New York, 1926; *Ancient Egyptian Religion*, Jaroslav Černý, London, 1952; *Myth and Symbol in Ancient Egypt*, R. T. Rundle Clark, New York, 1959; *The Ancient Egyptian Coffin Texts*, R. O. Faulkner, Warminster, Eng., 1973, 1977; *The Ancient Egyptian Pyramid Texts*, R. O. Faulkner, Oxford, 1969; *Images for Eternity*, Richard Fazzini, San Francisco/New York, 1975; *Ancient Egyptian Religion*, Henri Frankfort, New York, 1948; *Kingship and the Gods*, Henri Frankfort, Chicago, 1948; *X-raying the Pharaohs*, James E. Harris and Kent R. Weeks, New York, 1973; *Egyptian Mythology*, Veronica Ions, London, 1968; *Luxor: A Guide to Ancient Thebes*, Jill Kamil, London/New York, 1973; *Egyptian Religion*, Siegfried Morenz, Ithaca, N.Y., 1973; *Thebes of the Pharaohs*, Charles F. Nims, New York, 1965; *The Priests of Ancient Egypt*, Serge Sauneron, New York, 1960.

Change in a Changeless Land *Akhenaten and Nefertiti*, Cyril Aldred, London/New York, 1973; *Akhenaten, Pharaoh of Egypt*, Cyril Aldred, London/New York, 1968; *Treasures of Tutankhamun*, Metropolitan Museum, New York, 1976; *The Akhenaten Temple Project*, Ray Winfield Smith and Donald B. Redford, Warminster, Eng., 1976; *The Life and Times of Akhnaton*, Arthur Weigall, New York, 1923.

The Crest of Empire *The Warrior Pharaohs*, Leonard Cottrell, New York, 1969; *The World Saves Abu Simbel*, Christiane Desroches-Noblecourt and Georg Gerster, Vienna, 1968; "Egyptian Military Organization," R. O. Faulkner in the *Journal of Egyptian Archaeology*, Dec., 1953; *Everyday Life in Egypt in the Days of Ramses the Great*, Pierre Montet, London, 1962; *Lives of the Pharaohs*, Pierre Montet, Cleveland/New York, 1968; *History and Chronology of the 18th Dynasty of Egypt*, Donald B. Redford, Toronto, 1967; *Thebes in the Time of Amunhotep III*, Elizabeth Riefstahl, Norman, Okla., 1964; *When Egypt Ruled the East*, George Steindorff and Keith C. Seele, Chicago, 1957.

A number of periodicals carry articles that provide valuable reference material. Two devote their pages exclusively to Egyptology. They are the *Journal of Egyptian Archaeology*, published in London, and the *Journal of the American Research Center in Egypt*, Princeton. Other periodicals include: *Archaeology*, New York; *Antiquity*, Cambridge, Eng.; *Expedition*, Philadelphia; and the *American Journal of Archaeology*, New York. In addition, occasional pertinent articles appear in such publications as *Scientific American*, *Natural History*, *Science*, *National Geographic*, *Smithsonian*, *Illustrated London News*, and bulletins of major museums.

Illustration credits

In this listing picture sources are separated from left to right by a semicolon (;) and top to bottom by a dash (—). The following abbreviations are used:
EMC—Egyptian Museum, Cairo
MMA—Metropolitan Museum of Art, New York
BM—British Museum, London
BMFA—Boston Museum of Fine Arts
ht—height; dia—diameter; m—meter
cm—centimeter; ca—circa; col—column
NGP—National Geographic Photographer
NGS—National Geographic Staff
All dates given for Egyptian objects are B.C.

Cover Hieroglyphic reliefs from the shrine of Sesostris I at Karnak, ca 1971-1928: Farrell Grehan. Pages 2,3,7 Farrell Grehan.

The Constant Lure 8 Farrell Grehan. 10 through 15 From *Description de l'Égypte,* France, Commission des Monuments d'Égypte, Paris, 1809-1828. 16 From *Egyptian Obelisks* by Henry H. Gorringe, 1882. 17 From *Six New Plates. . . ,* by G. B. Belzoni, 1822, New York Public Library. 18 From *Century Illustrated Magazine,* May 1887—Radio Times Hulton Picture Library—From *Voyage dans la Haute Égypte,* by Auguste Mariette, 1893. 20,21 MMA: Harry Burton. 22 Griffith Institute, Ashmolean Museum, Oxford. 23 MMA: Harry Burton—Ledger Photo Service —MMA: Harry Burton. 24,25 MMA: Harry Burton. 26 Shrine doors, wood overlaid with gold, ht 50 cm, ca 1340, EMC: Fred J. Maroon. 27 Gilded wooden figure, ht 90 cm, ca 1340, EMC: Fred J. Maroon. 28,29 Gold funerary mask, ht 54 cm, ca 1340, EMC: John G. Ross. 30 Gold decorated dagger hilt, 12 cm long—Gilded leopard's head, ht 17 cm—Gold dagger and sheath, 32 cm long, all ca 1340, EMC: Lee Boltin. 31 Gold statuette, ht 5 cm; Gilded wooden serpent, ht 56 cm, both ca 1340, EMC: Lee Boltin

The People of the River 33 Painted clay figure, ht 29 cm, ca 4000, Brooklyn Museum—Terra-cotta vase, ht 22 cm, ca 3400, EMC—Flint and ivory knife, 23 cm long, ca 3100, Brooklyn Museum: all by Victor R. Boswell, Jr., NGP. 34,35 Front and back of slate palette, ht 64 cm, ca 3000, EMC: Victor R. Boswell, Jr., NGP. 36,37 Relief from the temple causeway of Unas, Saqqara, ca 2350: Victor R. Boswell, Jr., NGP—Farrell Grehan. 38 Lloyd K. Townsend, Jr. 39 Limestone relief, ht 45 cm, ca 1335, BMFA: Victor R. Boswell, Jr., NGP. 40,41 Wall painting from the tomb of Itat, 24x172 cm, ca 2570, EMC: Victor R. Boswell, Jr., NGP. 42,43 Farrell Grehan. 44,45 Farrell Grehan—Limestone relief in the tomb of Ti, Saqqara, ca 2400: Victor R. Boswell, Jr., NGP. 46,47 Farrell Grehan. 48,49 Thomas J. Abercrombie, NGS—Farrell Grehan. 50 through 55 Farrell Grehan. 56 Wooden statue of Kaaper, ht 109 cm, ca 2500; Painted limestone statue of the dwarf Seneb and family, ht 33 cm, ca 2350, both EMC: Victor R. Boswell, Jr., NGP. 57 Wooden statue of a Memphite couple, ht 69 cm, ca 2450, Louvre, Paris: Adam Woolfitt—Painted limestone statues of Rehotep and Nofret, ht 1.2 m, ca 2600, EMC, Joseph J. Scherschel, NGS. 58 Wooden model from the tomb of Meketre, base 1.7 m long, ca 2000, EMC: Victor R. Boswell, Jr., NGP. 59 Limestone relief in the tomb of Mereruka, Saqqara, ca 2300—Painted limestone relief, ca 2450, EMC: both Victor R. Boswell, Jr., NGP. 61 Limestone relief in the tomb of Ptahhotep, Saqqara, ca 2450—Limestone relief, ca 2450, Ägyptisches Museum, East Berlin: both Victor R. Boswell, Jr., NGP. 62,63 From *Ancient Egyptian Paintings* by Nina M. Davies and Alan H. Gardiner, courtesy The Oriental Institute, University of Chicago—Wall painting in the tomb of Menna, Thebes, ca 1400: Victor R. Boswell, Jr., NGP. 64 Wooden model from the tomb of Meketre, ht 29 cm, ca 2000, MMA—Limestone figure, woman making beer, ht 27 cm, ca 2450, EMC: Joseph J. Scherschel, NGS—Limestone figure, woman grinding grain, ht 28 cm, ca 2350, EMC: Victor R. Boswell, Jr., NGP. 64,65 Nathan Benn. 66,67 Wall relief in the tomb of Ptahhotep, Saqqara, ca 2450—wall painting in the tomb of Nakht, Thebes, ca 1410: both Victor R. Boswell, Jr., NGP. 68 Painted wall relief in the tomb of Ti, Saqqara, ca 2400: Victor R. Boswell, Jr., NGP. 69 Wall relief in the tomb of Nefer, Saqqara, ca 2400: Victor R. Boswell, Jr., NGP. 70,71 Farrell Grehan.

Pyramids: Building for Eternity 72 Farrell Grehan. 74 Limestone statue of Djoser, ht 1.4 m, ca 2650, EMC: Victor R. Boswell, Jr., NGP—Bronze statuette of Imhotep, ht 14 cm, BM: Gordon Roberton. 75,76 Farrell Grehan. 77 Lloyd K. Townsend, Jr. 78 Granite capstone, ht 1.4 m, ca 1800, EMC: Victor R. Boswell, Jr., NGP. 80,81 Farrell Grehan. 82 Schist triad of Mycerinus and goddesses, ht 95 cm, ca 2500, EMC: Victor R. Boswell, Jr., NGP. 83 Ivory statuette of Cheops, ht 8 cm, ca 2550—Diorite statue of Chephren, ht 1.7 m, ca 2525, both EMC: Victor R. Boswell, Jr., NGP. 84 Lloyd K. Townsend, Jr. 85 John G. Ross. 86,87 Farrell Grehan. 88 Rhind Papyrus, ca 1575, BM. 89 Fragment of a limestone relief, ca 1475, Brooklyn Museum; Wall relief in the tomb of Princess Idut, Saqqara, ca 2400: both by Victor R. Boswell, Jr., NGP. 90,91 Farrell Grehan; Copper and bronze tools (longest chisel 26 cm), EMC: Victor R. Boswell, Jr., NGP. 92 through 101 Michael A. Hampshire.

The Pleasures of Life 103 From *Ancient Egyptian Paintings* by Nina M. Davies and Alan H. Gardiner, courtesy The Oriental Institute, University of Chicago; Gold djed pillar ht 9 cm, ca 1340, EMC: Lee Boltin. 104 Wooden unguent spoon, 30 cm long, ca 1370, EMC: Victor R. Boswell, Jr., NGP. 105 Boxwood statuette, ht 13 cm, ca 1370, Gulbenkian Museum of Oriental Art, University of Durham, England. 106 Wooden toy animal, 13 cm long, ca 1300, BM: Gordon Roberton—Wooden "paddle doll," ht 22 cm, ca 2000, EMC: Victor R. Boswell, Jr., NGP. 106,107 From *Archaeological Survey of Egypt, Beni Hasan,* by Percy E. Newberry, 1894; Limestone statuette from the tomb of Nikauinpu, Giza, ht 21 cm, ca 2300, The Oriental Institute, University of Chicago: Robert M. Lightfoot III. 108,109 Comic papyrus, 54 cm long, ca 1000, BM. 111 Lloyd K. Townsend, Jr., based on a model in The Oriental Institute, University of Chicago. 112,113 Copy of a wall painting from the tomb of Ipuy, Thebes, ca 1250, MMA. 113 Wooden model from the tomb of Meketre, Thebes, 84 cm long, ca 2000, MMA, Rogers Fund—Fragment of a wall painting ca 1400, BM. 114,115 Reproduction of furniture from the tomb of Queen Hetepheres, Giza, chair ht 80 cm, bed 1.8 m long, ca 2600, BMFA: Victor R. Boswell, Jr., NGP. 116 Detail of a carved cedarwood chair, ht of chair 96 cm, ca 1340, EMC: Fred J. Maroon. 117 Ceremonial chair ht 1 m, ca 1340, EMC: Victor R. Boswell, Jr., NGP. 118 Painted wooden statue from the tomb of Methethy, ht 80 cm, ca 2450, Nelson Gallery-Atkins Museum, Kansas City, Mo.; Wooden sandals overlaid with bark, leather, and gold foil, ca 1340, EMC: Victor R. Boswell, Jr., NGP. 119 Painted wooden model from the tomb of Meketre, Thebes, ht 1.1 m, ca 2000; Crystalline limestone statue, ht 85 cm, ca 1330, both EMC: Victor R. Boswell, Jr., NGP. 120,121 Inlaid ebony chest, ht 37 cm, and cosmetic equipment (mirror is a reproduction), from the tomb of Sithathoryunet, ca 1880, hardwood comb, ca 1400, MMA; Limestone relief, from the sarcophagus of Kawit, ca 2040, EMC: Victor R. Boswell, Jr., NGP. 122 Gold and rock-crystal pendant, medallion dia 2 cm, ca 1900—Diadem of gold and semiprecious stones, ht 3 cm, ca 1900, both from the tomb of Princess Khnumet, EMC: Victor R. Boswell, Jr., NGP. 123 Inlaid gold headdress, ht 36 cm, ca 1450, MMA. 124,125 Collar of gold, carnelian, and feldspar from the tomb of Neferuptah, Hawara, 37 cm wide, ca 1800, EMC: Victor R. Boswell, Jr., NGP; Wall painting in the tomb of Nefertari, Thebes, ca 1250: Thomas J. Abercrombie, NGS—Rings of gold and semiprecious stones, ca 1340, EMC: Lee Boltin. 126 Bracelets of gold and lapis lazuli, 6 cm wide, ca 1250—Crown of gold and semiprecious stones, dia 19 cm, ca 1880, both EMC: Victor R. Boswell, Jr., NGP. 127 Pectoral of gold and silver with glass and semiprecious stones, ht 15 cm, ca 1340, EMC: Lee Boltin. 128,129 Wall painting in the tomb of Nakht, Thebes, ca 1410: Victor R. Boswell, Jr., NGP. 130 Painted relief in the tomb of Nefertari, Thebes, ca 1250—Wooden game, 28 cm long, ca 1295, EMC—Bone die, 2 cm wide, Coptic Period: all by Victor R. Boswell, Jr., NGP. 131 Ivory and ebony veneer game, 10x15 cm, with ivory playing pieces, from the tomb of Renseneb, ca 1795—Three knucklebones, both MMA. 132,133 Fragment of a wall painting, ca 1400, BM.—Ebony, copper, and gilt figure, ht 15 cm, ca 1425, Royal Scottish Museum, Edinburgh; Tableware, ca 1550-1300, MMA. 134,135 Fragment of a limestone relief, ht 50 cm, ca 1250, EMC: Victor R. Boswell, Jr., NGP. 136 Musical instruments, wood oboe (longest) 33 cm, ca 2000-300, Ägyptisches Museum, West Berlin: Victor R. Boswell, Jr., NGP. 137 Limestone relief from the tomb of Paatenemheb, Saqqara, ca 1340, Rijksmuseum van Oudheden, Leiden. 138,139 Painted relief in the tomb of Mehu, Saqqara, ca 2300: Victor R. Boswell, Jr., NGP.

The Gift of Writing 141 Painted limestone statue, ht 53 cm, ca 2500, Louvre, Paris: Pierre Boulat. 142,143 Painted relief in the tomb of Ti, Saqqara, ca 2400: Victor R. Boswell, Jr., NGP—Reconstructed scribe's writing kit, palette 7 cm long, The Oriental Institute, University of Chicago: Robert M. Lightfoot III. 144 Painting of Champollion by Madame Rumilly, 1823, courtesy the Champollion family. 145 Rosetta Stone, ht 1.1 m, ca 196, BM. 146 Detail from coffin lid of wood and glass, ca 350, EMC: Victor R. Boswell, Jr., NGP. 147 Details from sarcophagus in the tomb of Amunhotep II, Thebes, ca 1410: Victor R. Boswell, Jr., NGP. 148 Painted wall relief in the tomb of Nefer, Saqqara, ca 2400, Victor R. Boswell, Jr., NGP—Robert Hynes—Papyrus Institute, Cairo. 149 Farrell Grehan. 150 From the Edwin Smith Surgical Papyrus, ca 1700, New York Academy of Medicine Library. 151 Papyrus letter with mud seal, 8 cm long, ca 2000, MMA—Tutankhamun's ivory palette with brushes and wood case overlaid with gold, both 30 cm long, ca 1340, EMC: F. L Kenett from Robert Harding Associates—Tutankhamun's ivory and gold burnisher, 16 cm long, ca 1340, EMC: Lee Boltin. 152 Steatite scarab, 9 cm long, ca 1390, MMA, Rogers Fund. 153 Victor R. Boswell, Jr., NGP.

Pathways to the Gods 155 Detail, wall painting in the tomb of Pashedu, Thebes, ca 1150: Victor R. Boswell, Jr., NGP. 156 Tomb of Mereruka, Saqqara, ca 2350: Victor R. Boswell, Jr., NGP. 157 Wall painting in the tomb of Irinufer, Thebes, ca 1200: Victor R. Boswell, Jr., NGP. 158,159 Cedarwood boat, 43 cm long, ca 2550: John G. Ross. 160,161 Ceiling painting in the tomb of Seti I, Thebes, ca 1290: Victor R. Boswell, Jr., NGP. 162,163 Ceiling painting in the tomb of Ramses VI, Thebes, ca 1150: Victor R. Boswell, Jr., NGP. 164,165 Robert Hynes. 166,167 Lloyd K. Townsend, Jr. 168 through 179 Farrell Grehan. 180 Bronze cat, ht 37 cm, ca 600; Gold falcon head, ht 35 cm, ca 1900, both EMC: Victor R. Boswell, Jr., NGP. 181 Gold figurine, ht 6 cm, ca 700, BMFA; Blue faience hippopotamus, ht 10 cm, ca 1900—Bronze mongoose, ht 20 cm, ca 500, both EMC: all Victor R. Boswell, Jr., NGP—Bronze crocodile, ht 12 cm, ca 200, BM: 182,183 Painted reliefs in the Temple of Seti I, Abydos, ca 1290: Victor R. Boswell, Jr., NGP. 184,185 Painted relief in the Temple of Amun-Re, Karnak, ca 320: Farrell Grehan. 186,187 Farrell Grehan. 188,189 Detail, wall painting in the tomb of Ramose, Thebes, ca 1360: Thomas J. Abercrombie, NGS; Detail, wall painting in the tomb of Ramose, Thebes, ca 1360: Victor R. Boswell, Jr., NGP. 190,191 Farrell Grehan. 192,193 Wall painting in the tomb of Sennedjem, Thebes, ca 1200—Ushabtis, ht of tallest 24 cm, ca 1560 to 300, Ägyptisches Museum, West Berlin: both Victor R. Boswell, Jr., NGP. 194 Mummy of Ramses II, ca 1220, EMC: Nathan Benn. 195 Wall painting in the tomb of Sennedjem, Thebes, ca 1200—Alabaster canopic jars, average ht 38 cm, EMC: both Victor R. Boswell, Jr., NGP. 196,197 from the Hunefer papyrus scroll, ca 1290, BM. 198,199 Painted relief in the tomb of Seti I, Thebes, ca 1290: Victor R. Boswell, Jr., NGP. 200,201 Victor R. Boswell, Jr., NGP.

Change in a Changeless Land 202 Crystalline limestone relief, ht 1 m, ca 1350, EMC: Victor R. Boswell, Jr., NGP. 203 Fragment of a limestone relief, ht 23 cm, ca 1350, BMFA: Victor R. Boswell, Jr., NGP. 204 Limestone relief, ca 1350, Brooklyn Museum: Victor R. Boswell, Jr., NGP. 205 Drawing on limestone, ca 1350, EMC; Limestone relief, ca 1350, Brooklyn Museum, Charles Edwin Wilbour Fund: both Victor R. Boswell, Jr., NGP. 207 Painted wooden head of Tutankhamun, ht 30 cm, ca 1340, EMC: Fred J. Maroon; Painted yew wood head, ht 10 cm, ca 1370—Limestone stela, ht 33 cm, ca 1350, both Ägyptisches Museum, West Berlin: Victor R. Boswell, Jr., NGP. 208,209 From *Tell el Amarna,* by W. M. Flinders Petrie, 1894. 210 Quartzite head, ht 33 cm, ca 1350, EMC: Victor R. Boswell, Jr., NGP. 211 Sandstone statue of Akhenaten, ht 4 m, ca 1350, EMC: Victor R. Boswell, Jr., NGP. 212,213 From *Ancient Egyptian Paintings* by Nina M. Davies and Alan H. Gardiner, courtesy The Oriental Institute, University of Chicago; Quartzite head, ht 21 cm, ca 1350, EMC: Lee Boltin. 214,215 Reliefs from a temple wall, ca 1350, Luxor Museum: Victor R. Boswell, Jr., NGP. 216,217 Back panel of the throne of Tutankhamun, wood overlaid with gold and inlays, ht 53 cm, ca 1340, EMC: Lee Boltin. 218 Alabaster perfume vase, ht 70 cm, ca 1340, EMC: Victor R. Boswell, Jr., NGP. 219 Alabaster vase, 38 cm long; Alabaster lion jar, ht 60 cm, both ca 1340, EMC: Fred J. Maroon. 220,221 Ostrich fan, ht 10 cm, ca 1340, EMC: Fred J. Maroon.

The Crest of Empire 222 Indurated limestone statue of Hatshepsut, ht 2 m, ca 1485, MMA, Rogers Fund. 223 Painted wall relief from the temple of Hatshepsut, Deir el Bahri, ca 1485, EMC: Victor R. Boswell, Jr., NGP. 224 Lloyd K. Townsend, Jr. 225 Basalt statue of Thutmose III, ht 89 cm, ca 1450, Luxor Museum: Victor R. Boswell, Jr., NGP. 226,227

Bentwood chariot overlaid with gold, 2.1 m wide, ca 1340, EMC: Victor R. Boswell, Jr., NGP. 228 Wall relief from the tomb of Horemheb, Saqqara, ca 1340, Rijksmuseum van Oudheden, Leiden. 229 Granite statue of Horemheb, ht 1.1 m, ca 1340, MMA, Gift of Mr. and Mrs. Everett Macy, 1923. 230,231 Copy of a painted wall relief from the temple of Ramses II at Beit el Wali, BM—Granite statue of Ramses II as a child, ht 2.3 m, ca 1280, EMC: Victor R. Boswell, Jr., NGP. 232,233 Wall relief from the temple of Ramses II at Abu Simbel, ca 1260: Farrell Grehan. 234 Wall relief in the temple of Ramses III, Medinet Habu, ca 1170: Victor R. Boswell, Jr., NGP—Relief on the base of a colossus at Abu Simbel, ca 1260: Farrell Grehan. 235 Wall relief in the temple of Ramses II at Abu Simbel, ca 1260: Farrell Grehan. 236,237 Painted wooden models from the tomb of Mesehti, Thebes, ht 40 cm, base 2 m long, ca 2000, EMC: Victor R. Boswell, Jr., NGP. 238 through 243 Farrell Grehan.

Time Chart 244 Col 2 Pottery vase, ht 25 cm, Ägyptisches Museum, West Berlin—Pottery pig, ht 26 cm, Ankara Archeological Museum, Turkey: Ara Guler. Col 3 Bird deity, ht 29 cm, Brooklyn Museum: Victor R. Boswell, Jr., NGP—Stamp seal, ht 4 cm, Los Angeles County Museum, Heeremaneck Collection: Edith Porada—Gold ornament, ht 6 cm, Archaeological Museum, Varna, Bulgaria: Erich Lessing, Magnum. Col 4 Gerzean vase, ht 22 cm, EMC: Victor R. Boswell, Jr., NGP—Sumerian clay pictograph tablet, Louvre, Paris. 245 Col 1 Narmer palette, ht 64 cm, EMC: Victor R. Boswell, Jr., NGP—Maltese figurine, ht 48 cm, National Museum of Malta: Adam Woolfitt.

Col 2 Limestone funerary stela, Louvre, Paris: John G. Ross—Silver bull vase from Iran, ht 16 cm, MMA, Joseph Pulitzer Bequest, 1966. Col 3 Step Pyramid: Farrell Grehan—Detail from the Standard of Ur, BM—Stonehenge: W. E. Roscher. Col 4 The Great Sphinx: Farrell Grehan—Ebla tablet, ht 10 cm: Gianni Tortolli—Steatite figure, National Museum of Pakistan, Karachi: Josephine Powell. 246 Col 1 Tomb of Mereruka: Victor R. Boswell, Jr., NGP—Bronze head, ht 30 cm, Iraq Museum, Baghdad: Joseph J. Scherschel, NGS. Col 2 Relief from sarcophagus of Kawit, EMC: Victor R. Boswell, Jr., NGP—Green calcite statue of Gudea, ht 63 cm, Louvre, Paris: Adam Woolfitt. Col 3 Shrine of Sesostris I: Farrell Grehan—Cycladic marble statuette, National Museum, Athens. Col 4 Quartzite statue of a nobleman, ht 70 cm, Brooklyn Museum, Charles Edwin Wilbour Fund: Victor R. Boswell, Jr., NGP—Minoan faience "snake goddess," ht 29 cm, Archeological Museum of Herakleion, Crete: Gilbert M. Grosvenor, NGS. 247 Col 1 Head of limestone statue, MMA, Rogers Fund and contribution of Edward S. Harkness, 1929—Gold Mycenaean mask, ht 26 cm, National Archaeological Museum, Athens: Gordon Gahan, NGP. Col 2 Limestone bust of Nefertiti, ht 58 cm, Ägyptisches Museum, West Berlin: Victor R. Boswell, Jr., NGP—Lion Gate, Mycenae: Gordon Gahan, NGP—Bronze wine vessel, ht 20 cm: Robert Harding Associates, Times Newspapers, Ltd. Col 3 Wall painting in the tomb of Pashedu, Thebes: Thomas J. Abercrombie, NGS—Clay warrior vase, ht 36 cm, National Museum, Athens, Prothmann Associates—Tlatilco figurine, ht 8 cm, National Museum of Anthropology,

Mexico City: B. Anthony Stewart. Col 4 Gold triad of gods, ht 9 cm, Louvre, Paris: Adam Woolfitt—Nora stone, Museum of Archeology, Cagliari, Sardinia: Winfield Parks—Olmec head, ht 2.7 m, National Museum of Anthropology, Mexico City: B. Anthony Stewart. 248 Col 1 Black granite bust of Mentuemhat, ht 48 cm, EMC: Mario Carrieri—Ivory "Mona Lisa of Nimrud," ht 16 cm, Iraq Museum, Baghdad: Hirmer Fotoarchiv. Col 2 Bronze cat, EMC: Victor R. Boswell, Jr., NGP—Warrior frieze from Persepolis, Iran: Helen and Frank Schreider—Detail of an Etruscan terra-cotta sculpture on a sarcophagus, Museo Nationale di Villa Giulia, Rome: Dan McCoy, Black Star. Col 3 Alabaster lion vessel, ht 11 cm, Brooklyn Museum, Charles Edwin Wilbour Fund—Parthenon, Athens: Franc Shor—Ceramic pot, ht 18 cm, Museum of the American Indian, New York. Col 4 Green schist head, ht 15 cm, Brooklyn Museum, Charles Edwin Wilbour Fund—Thracian coin, dia 3 cm: Helen and Frank Schreider. 249 Col 1 Granite statue of falcon god Horus at Edfu, ht 3 m: Farrell Grehan—Marble "Winged Victory of Samothrace," ht 2.5 m, Louvre, Paris: Marc Garanger—Head of life-size terra-cotta statue, China Pictorial. Col 2 Rosetta Stone, ht 1.1 m, BM—Marble "Venus de Milo," Louvre, Paris: Bruce Dale, NGP—Clay head, ht 8 cm, Ohio Historical Society, Columbus: Robert S. Oakes, NGP. Col 4 Temple of Hathor at Dendera: Anne Dirkes Kobor, NGS—Detail of a life-size marble statue of Julius Caesar, City Council Chamber, Rome: Adam Woolfitt—Embroidered figure, National Museum of Anthropology and Archeology, Lima: Loren McIntyre.

Index

Type composition by National Geographic's Photographic Services. Color separations by Colorgraphics, Inc., Forestville, Md.; Chanticleer Company, Inc., New York, N. Y.; Progressive Color Corporation, Rockville, Md.; J. Wm. Reed Company, Alexandria, Va. Printing by Fawcett Printing Corporation, Rockville, Md.; Judd & Detweiler, Inc., Washington, D. C.; Kingsport Press, Kingsport, Tenn. Binding by R. R. Donnelley & Sons Company, Chicago, Ill.; Rand McNally & Company, Skokie, Ill. Paper by Mead Corp., Publishing Paper Division, New York, N. Y. Papyrus from the Papyrus Institute, Cairo, Egypt.

Library of Congress CIP Data

Main entry under title:

Ancient Egypt, Discovering its Splendors

Bibliography: p.
Includes index.
1. Egypt—Civilization—To 332 B.C. I. National Geographic Society, Washington, D. C.
DT61.A6   932   78-10524
ISBN 0-87044-220-1